HOW TO
RECORD
YOUR OWN
MUSIC AND
GET IT ON
THE INTERNET

D1472209

HOW TO RECORD YOUR OWN MUSIC AND GET IT ON THE INTERNET

Leo Coulter and
Richard Jones

CHARTWELL
BOOKS, INC.

A QUARTO BOOK

Published in 2009 by
CHARTWELL BOOKS, INC.
A division of BOOK SALES, INC.
276 Fifth Avenue Suite 206
New York, New York 10001
USA

ISBN-13: 978-0-7858-2588-3
ISBN-10: 0-7858-2588-6

QUAR.HCR

This book was designed
and produced by
Quarto Publishing plc
The Old Brewery
6 Blundell Street
London N7 9BH

Project editor: Liz Dalby
Art editor: Louise Clements
Illustrations: John Woodcock
Art director: Caroline Guest

Creative director: Moira Clinch
Publisher: Paul Carslake

Printed by Midas Printing
International Ltd, China
Color separation by Pica Digital Pte Ltd,
Singapore

Contents

Introduction

The basic form and instrumentation of your song has to be in place before you start recording. Of course, things will change during the recording process, but walking into the studio with a mere chord progression or two is a waste of everyone's time.

You want to present your music to the world in the most attractive way possible. There are plenty of magazines, books, and websites out there that are aware of this, and they can't wait to tell you how easy it is to record your own music these days. Just look at all the affordable equipment out there! What's stopping you from creating a great-sounding demo or even a fully-fledged album? Tools that were the preserve of high-end recording studios just 20 years ago are now available to everyone for a modest outlay. Those encouraging magazines, books, and websites are right; there really has never been a better time to record your own music.

There are some strange contradictions inherent to the idea that DIY recording is quite as wonderful as some people would have us believe, though. For example, the digital technology upon which modern home recording is based is supposed to have improved the quality of recorded music dramatically, yet many of the finest recordings ever produced predate the existence of digital technology and computer editing altogether. On the other hand, it is true that countless commercially successful records are now recorded in people's homes. But where are they mixed and mastered, and by whom?

Music released by record companies is rarely—if ever—a DIY job in its entirety. The corporate music industry still relies on sound, mix, and mastering engineers who work in high-end studios to give records a competitive edge. The discerning musician who has been promised fully professional results from a typical low- to mid-priced home studio setup is likely to feel confused

This book is aimed at those who demand the best possible presentation of their music.

Getting it out there
Recording your music will make it accessible to an ever-increasing audience.

and frustrated that his recordings don't bear comparison with the professionally produced albums he most admires.

Not every musician is a discerning musician by these standards, and there are many musicians who will be satisfied by their early efforts at multitrack recording. This book is not for them. This book is aimed at those who demand the best possible presentation of their music, who want to communicate their ideas to their audience in a clear, effective, and appealing way,

whether they are producing a demo, an EP, or a full album. This means understanding the recording, mixing, and mastering processes, while being able to successfully present and market your music online once the recording process is over. A tall order, but we're here to help.

This book will advise you on the best way to record real-life singers and instruments, and it will explain how you can shape your recording into an effective piece of music that can be shared on the internet. There is a thrill to a recorded performance that

Staying ahead
The recording of real-time, real-world performances will give your music the edge.

really "happened"; it affects the listener in a way that freeze-dried samples and loops never can. We want to encourage you to discover the joys and avoid the pitfalls of home recording; we want you to produce fantastic sounds that are entirely your own. Samples have their place, of course, especially in pop, hip-hop, and other genres in which the use of drum machines is de rigueur. However, even samples will be more effective if you record them yourself. We believe that the recording of real-time, real-world performances is the method most likely to lift your music above the inferior efforts of your

competitors and get you noticed!

One thing you will notice about this book is its unusual approach to evaluating recording equipment, an approach quite at odds with the way studio gear is usually reviewed. For one thing, software EQ and compressor plug-ins are not reviewed alongside hardware EQs and compressors. This is not because the authors of this book are old-school analogphiles who love all things retro and shun the use of computers. Far from it. Our decision not to comment on a number of popular products—such as certain brands of Chinese-made microphones and

More than anything else, we hope that this book will help you express yourself.

the plethora of inexpensive one-size-fits-all integrated recording solutions on the market—has nothing to do with snobbery and everything to do with helping the reader to avoid squandering a precious recording budget on equipment that is, at best, merely adequate.

On the other hand, our decision not to review plug-in EQs and compressors is not a comment on the quality and usefulness of plug-ins; it is a reflection of the outstanding quality of plug-ins that are already included in your recording software! The default channel EQ and compressor in Logic, for example, are so impressive and versatile that it makes sense to supplement these with hardware EQs and compressors if anything. Hardware signal processors are more likely to offer character, presence, and something different to your music, and we feel strongly that a few

good pieces of outboard will benefit your mixes more than a variety of third-party plug-ins. Good analog hardware also has excellent resale value and it won't become out-of-date, making it a good long-term investment compared to plug-ins and software.

More than anything else, we hope this book will help you to express yourself, and that your music will become accessible to an ever-increasing audience as your recording, mixing, and self-promotion skills develop. As major record labels continue to struggle and the likelihood of signing a record deal decreases for all musicians, your ability to fulfill several different roles in the production and marketing of your music will become more and more important. Here's what you need to know...

About this book

This book takes you from the basics of getting your act together, through understanding, selecting, and setting up equipment, to recording your music and manipulating it to achieve a professional-sounding result. Finally there are sections on getting your music on the web, outstanding albums to listen to for inspiration, and a glossary of all the technical terms used in the book.

Helpful text
The detailed text is packed with insider information and insights.

Pro tips
Issues to consider are highlighted, as well as simple ways around common problems.

Band name and image

Coming up with a good band name is an art in itself. You need to find a name that's original, catchy and—most importantly—not already taken

Stage name
Whether you're a solo artist or in a group, sometimes you won't be happy with your birth name and you'll want something a bit more exciting. While you don't need to change your name legally, you might want to toy with the idea of a stage name. It's a lot more common than you might think.

A stage name might simply omit your last name (such as Madonna or Beyoncé) or be an alternative spelling of your name (such as James Marshall "Jimi" Hendrix). You could, however, consider completely reinventing your name like the following artists:

BIRTH NAME	STAGE NAME
Stefani Germanotta	Lady Gaga
Robert Zimmerman	Bob Dylan
Richard Starkey	Ringo Starr
Timothy Mosley	Timbaland

Doppelganger alert!
Naturally, you'll want your band or act to have a unique name. This is, however, not easy to achieve, as there are literally millions of unsigned acts all over the globe. Indeed, you might have already come across another unsigned act on the internet with your name. This is nothing to worry about at this stage; it only becomes an issue if either of you become so successful that anyone else using the same name could be accused of profiting from false association with

a crowd-pulling brand or identity. And if both of you become successful, you could hurt each other's reputation. The 1970s rock band Blue, for example, sued UK 1990s boy band Blue for allegedly damaging their career. Even song names aren't safe: the Red Hot Chili Peppers, for example, sued TV show "Californication" for identity theft. In short, make sure you don't clash with any successful names!

Image
If you think your act is "just about the music," you're fooling yourself. Fully-formed artists come as a stylistic whole that includes sonic identity, clothes, color schemes, favored geometric shapes, and cultural allegiances. The

CHOOSING A NAME
A good band name should:
• Be easy to say, read, and spell
• Be short and memorable
• Have interesting or amusing double meanings that work with your music

A dubious band name might:
• Be complicated or convoluted
• Be difficult to pronounce or spell
• Accidentally mean something inappropriate in another language
• Have obscure double meanings that don't correspond with your act

---

International appeal!
Queen had huge international appeal. Their short, simple, memorable name can't have hurt

23

Band name and image

CASE STUDY: QUEEN
It is hard to find a more successful choice of band name than "Queen." It's a short, memorable, everyday word that also connotes two very different, equally evocative ideas: royalty

and homosexuality. Its lead singer Freddie Mercury, who came up with the name, was also a trained graphic illustrator and designed the famous Queen crest. He was so conscious of

the presentation and marketing of his act that he also legally changed his name (from Farrokh Bulsara) around the time Queen was formed.

Practical advice
Solutions are offered to suit a range of situations and budgets.

Panels
Key points are pulled out of the main text and summarized.

Case studies
Real examples of artists are used throughout, giving you an instant point of reference.

Compressors buyer's guide

A selection of compressors to suit all budgets and a description of each compressor's characteristic sound.

Symetrix 501
• **Mono**
• **Budget**
The Symetrix 501 is a good-value compressor that's quiet, fully featured (there's auto release, a sidechain function, and you can link two of them together for stereo operation), and versatile. It excels at compressing bass guitar and drums and you'll be amazed at how cheaply you can pick one up if you look around.

Chameleon Labs 7720
• **Stereo**
• **Mid-priced**
The 7720 is a stereo VCA compressor designed for the mix-bus. This sort of compressor won't impose its own character on a mix, so if you want one that imparts its own color,

look elsewhere. The 7720 excels at transparent, low-ratio compression that "glues" a mix together as well as drum-bus and acoustic guitar compression.

Universal Audio 1176LN
• **Mono**
• **Expensive**
Universal Audio 1176LN is an FET compressor (strictly speaking, a limiter) that imparts a warm and distinctive "it sounds like a record!" sound to whatever is passed through it. Use it on vocals, bass, electric guitar, kick drum, room mic—just about anywhere.

Manley Vari-Mu
• **Stereo**
• **Mid-priced**
Mastering engineers are probably the most

demanding customers in pro-audio land. The Manley Vari-Mu is a very popular mastering audio compressor and it has been a bestseller for Manley (who make exclusively high-end gear) for a number of years. The circuit configuration is similar to the rare mid-costly Fairchild 670.

FMR Really Nice Compressor
• **Stereo**
• **Budget**
The RNC isn't your usual budget stereo compressor. By coupling digital controls with an all-analog signal path and a "SuperNice" mode that replicates the artifact-free, transparent compression of three compressors processing a signal in series, FMR have made a powerful, versatile, and inexpensive compressor that is within everyone's financial reach.

DBX 160X
• **Mono**
• **Mid-priced**
DBX no longer make the 160X (or XT) compressor, which is a

Art Pro VLA II

sharne because quite a few sound engineers prefer it to DBX's current model, the 160A. If you search the secondhand market for this, you might find an outstanding bass guitar and snare drum compressor at a very attractive price.

ART Pro VLA II
• **Stereo**
• **Budget**
The VLA uses "Vactrol" optical electronics and a 12AT7 vacuum-tube gain stage to create a sound that is all its own; it's such a natural-sounding compressor that it can achieve great results on voice or piano, as well as on overheads and synths.

Chandler TG1
• **Stereo**
• **Expensive**
The custom EMI recording consoles from the late 1960s incorporated the TG12413 limiter that has been recreated by Chandler as the TG1.

compressor: The TG1 sounds particularly fabulous when extreme settings are used and source material is "squashed" with a low threshold and high ratio.

Joe Meek SC2
• **Stereo**
• **Mid-priced**
Pioneering record producer Joe Meek is often credited as being the first sound engineer to realize the full potential of compression as an effect rather than a mere tool for the regulation of dynamics. "Joe Meek" the company has made compression as an effect its specialty and the SC2 (particularly its earlier revisions 1.05 and 1.07) is probably the ultimate "effect" compressor. A photo-optical design, when pushed hard it can alter the tone and rhythm of your tracks and do something different than the other compressors in your rack or DAW.

Inner Tube Audio Atomic Squeezebox
• **Stereo**
• **Fantasy island**
The Atomic Squeezebox takes unobtrusive, transparent compression to a whole new level thanks to a unique design that does not incorporate VCAs, FETs, optical, variable-Mu, or any method of gain reduction the world has ever seen before! There's no pumping, no coloration, no changing the balance of the mix or introducing unwanted artifacts—Inner Tube likes it to having a rack-mounted assistant engineer riding the faders for you!

Chameleon Labs 7720

7720

SEE ALSO The signal chain 32 Polar patterns 42

How do microphones work?

Microphones transduce (change) sound into electrical energy, and they do so in two stages.

1 Turning vibrating air into vibrating metal: the diaphragm
An ultra-thin suspended diaphragm in the microphone capsule vibrates in response to incoming sound waves. (Imagine a miniature round sail flapping backward and forward in temperamental winds, then speed it up.) The diaphragm is either made of metal itself or is coupled to a vibrating element made of metal. It's made of metal because metal conducts electricity and air doesn't, and an electrical signal can only be extracted from a material that's conductive.

How the diaphragm is suspended and housed in the microphone determines how well it can pick up incoming sound from different directions—this is called its *pickup* or *polar pattern* (see page 42).

2 Turning vibrating metal into an electrical signal: transduction
So now the piece of metal is fluttering in the sonic wind... but this fluttering needs to be turned into electricity. What's needed is some kind of force-field that can extract electrical "meaning" from the moving conductor. Different mics use different fields and electronic components to achieve this. The method used determines the microphone type (see page 46).

Tech talk

Large, medium, or small
Large diaphragms—⅞ in (18 mm) or larger—are very sensitive, but also add a fair bit of coloration to your sound. They are traditionally used for a "big" sound, particularly on vocals. Small diaphragms, on the other hand, are lighter and faster, and so capture transients and high frequencies better, adding brightness and definition to the sound. These diaphragms are generally considered to be ⅝ in (15 mm) or smaller. A happy medium between small and large is the medium-sized diaphragm, which exhibits a combination of both the "big" and the "clear" characteristics.

How a microphone works
This cutaway shows the component parts of a typical diaphragm microphone.

Soundwaves make diaphragm vibrate

Magnetic coil

Wires carry electric signal

PROTECTING YOUR MICROPHONE
Diaphragms are sensitive little things. Shaking stands and flowing air (displaced air from a heavy-footed drummer's kick drum, for example, or a singer breathing directly into the microphone) can force the diaphragm to vibrate heavily, resulting in unwanted noise on your recording. To stop unwanted airflow, mesh or foam "windscreens" are provided with most microphones. In addition, you can use pop shields when recording vocals to avoid "popping" on consonants with explosive airflow (such as "p," "b," "t," "d"),

and "t"). Shock mounts suspend a microphone inside a metal frame so that it effectively floats when the mic stand is knocked or shaken.

Chapter 1

Getting started

 Every great artist needs inspiration. But a great artist also needs an orderly, functional environment in which to work. It's essential to be prepared and well organized from the very beginning of your career as a self-produced musician.

Here's how to do it...

Getting your act together

If you want to record your own music successfully, you
need to be able to envision your songs and style clearly.
Of course there's equipment to buy and a studio to set up,
but nothing should distract you from the preparation
of your music, which is of prime importance.

Musicianship and recording used
to be completely separate affairs.
These days they blend into one
another, and it's easy for the process
of songwriting and recording to
become a bit sloppy as a result.
This chapter will help you to isolate
the factors that demand careful
consideration before you start
recording your songs properly.

Ensemble playing

"Way back when," musicians
had little or no knowledge of the
technicalities of sound recording,
and they would spend very little time
in the studio. When they did perform
there, they still had to play as an
ensemble because overdubbing and
sophisticated tape editing hadn't
been invented yet.

Digital assembly
*Nowadays, many musicians and composers
explore musical ideas through samples and
overdubbing on their computer, rather than
by playing together.*

ARE YOU READY?
*Preparation is everything.
In the case of home
recording, it's vital that:*
- *Your songs are finished.
  This means lyrics, basic
  instrumentation, and
  all sections should be
  complete, at least in a
  "first draft" form.*
- *You and the other
  musicians who will*
*feature in the recording
can play the material.*
- *You have an idea of
  how you want your songs
  to be produced.*
- *You have a name and
  a general idea of what
  genre and ethos your
  act falls into.*
- *You have a space where
  you can set up a home
  recording studio.*

Ensemble playing
Ensemble playing depended on rehearsal. Count Basie was regarded as one of the great jazz band leaders.

Song logistics

While fine-tuning your composition, it's wise to bear in mind the demands that the structure and arrangement of your song are going to make on the recording process.

1 Number of instruments
The number of instruments that appear on your track makes a huge difference to the practical difficulty of recording. An unaccompanied guitarist/singer/songwriter, for example, will require hardly any recording space and the use of as few as two microphones. A traditional big band of ten or more players with bulky trombones and saxophones, on the other hand, will need a recording room the size of a school gym and countless microphones and recording channels. Even if you record all members separately and overdub them, you will have avoided having to hire a huge room but you will have spent about ten times as long recording the ensemble! Whatever route you take, more instruments means more time, and often more cost. And remember: if you bring in session musicians that aren't part of your core band, they'll want to get paid… by the hour.

Anticipate problems
When writing a song, try to anticipate logistical problems from the outset.

CASE STUDIES
Bohemian Rhapsody (Queen)
This world-famous song possesses a middle section that was so ridiculously complex to record back in 1975 that it reportedly became the most expensive and time-consuming

recording to date, involving five different music studios. The composition demanded an extensive "operatic" section (with up to 180 vocal overdubs) that took over three weeks to record. Fortunately, Queen had the time, money, and determination to pull it off.

Frank Zappa, the tragic perfectionist
Zappa's compositional ambitions often exhausted the patience and resources of the record companies and musicians he worked with. On his debut album, The Mothers of Invention's "Freak Out!," the track

2 Level of technical difficulty

The harder something is to play or sing, the longer it will take to get it right in rehearsal and the more likely you are to require multiple takes before you get a "keeper." Musically ambitious material can take weeks to record (see Case studies, below), and can easily degenerate into a demoralizing experience with an unfinished recording. Be wary of this possibility, and know your musicians' limits as well as your own.

3 Length

It sounds obvious, but the longer your song, the more needs to be recorded. Be sure that you've got enough time for those quirky middle sections, expansive solos, and lengthy codas. Recording always takes longer than you think, so if in doubt, cut the song down.

4 Number of sections

Different sections can multiply the time needed to record a song. If you have a song with two distinct sonic or musical worlds for chorus and verse, for example, you're essentially recording two songs, each with different microphone positions,

instruments, musical textures, and rhythms. Be sure that you want such multi-dimensionality, and allow twice as much time for recording if you do.

KICKING OUT THE EGOS

Admittedly, this has nothing to do with song structure, but since we're discussing logistics and the practicalities of home recording we might as well address the biggest potential pitfall of the recording process: the personality clash! There's only one way to prepare for this eventuality, and that is to tell every person involved with the recording process to leave his or her ego at the front door. It might not work, but at least you can say you tried...

"The Return of the Son of Monster Magnet" wasn't allowed the necessary time and money to be finished, and on "London Symphony Orchestra," the under-rehearsed pieces were so far off Zappa's vision that even after weeks of painstaking editing he still felt obliged to admit in the liner notes that it was "infested with wrong notes and out-of-tune passages." Unreliable and disinterested session musicians plagued much of Zappa's career, although a notable exception is "The Yellow Shark," which is worth listening to simply for the rare harmony between composer and performers that characterizes the recording.

Song preparation

The basic form and instrumentation of your song has to be in place before you start recording. Of course, things will change during the recording process, but walking into the studio with a mere chord progression or two is a waste of everyone's time.

Writing as you record

Some songwriters like to lay down sketches of their songs on simple multitrack recording setups where the sound and performance quality are relatively unimportant. This technique can act as a brilliant preparation for the recording proper (Jeff Buckley's four-track sketches are a good example—see Playlist, page 170). If you're the songwriter in the band, for example, often the best way to show your collaborators what your song is about is knocking up a rough demo prior to the recording sessions.

Structure as scaffolding

Consider your draft a necessary starting point, or scaffolding, to

the finished product. The aim of your sketch is not to rob the recording of musical spontaneity, and there's no reason why you should strictly adhere to it. But you need a rough map of the song before you're able to move things around and improvise in the studio.

A sketch will give you an idea of logistics; how many tracks you're likely to use, what kind of sound you might be after, and what instruments you'll be recording, how many session players you might need, and how much space you'll need in your live area.

Another major reason for having a basic song structure in place is

---

SONG SKETCH CHECKLIST

A rough sketch of a song should give an idea of the following:

- *Time signature and tempo—knowing the BPM ballpark and being clear about your beats per measure are absolutely essential for musicians and producers alike.*
- *Structure—intro, verse, chorus, middle-eight, solo, and any other sections*

need to be accounted for, including the order in which they appear, and their duration.

- *Arrangement—your sketch should give a basic indication of the material that will be played by different instruments, what instruments are playing what in different sections, and so on.*

Don't confuse laying down first drafts of songs with

laying down the finished product, so save your serious recording efforts—complete with heavy-duty outboard gear, carefully selected miking positions and the full band's attendance—for when a song is ready. Otherwise you'll probably waste everyone's time figuring out what the song actually is while running up a frightening electricity bill.

Keep it simple

Writing a part that is on the edge of your technical ability is a bad idea. Where possible, keep things simple.

that all your musicians will have had a chance to learn their parts. Performers need to know what they're doing. The longer they've had to practice any particular part, the better they're going to be at it. They'll be more confident technically and able to add flair to their performance as a result, which means you have to spend less time cutting and pasting bad takes together into a barely adequate one.

Simplification

If, after much practice, your musicians are still uncomfortable with the music, consider simplifying the parts. Nothing sounds more embarrassing than musicians punching above their weight, especially on a record, where there's really no excuse for feeble playing! Luckily, stripped-down instrumentations and vocals have been considered "cool" since the punk movement in the late 1970s, so

you certainly won't forsake any of your integrity. Coolness aside, simplifying musical material can actually make for an interesting version of your song that you might end up preferring.

Rehearsal

Just as it's important to practice separately, it's equally vital to rehearse together before entering the studio. Even if you choose to record each instrument one at a time, it's good for a player to appreciate where her or his part fits into the arrangement. Greater awareness of context means a performance more in keeping with the spirit of the song as a whole.

If you're thinking of tinkering with your song, this is when to do it. In rehearsal, the band can interact spontaneously, ideas can be shared quickly, and the song's sections and parts can develop and grow. Developing your material with all musicians present will most likely produce more enjoyable results than endless cutting and pasting on your DAW.

Your act

Whether you're a heavy metal band or a folk singer/songwriter, your act needs some definition and vision before you start recording.

Genre

Most acts despise being pigeonholed, but that's exactly what everyone's going to be doing to your music, especially at the beginning when they might have heard only 30 seconds of a song. Ordinarily, resisting classification of your music would be unhelpful to the process of producing and exposing it. Most acts start out as genre acts to some degree and only with increasing commercial success can they afford to hone a signature style. This is particularly true when it comes to album productions.

What kind of production?

Genre plays an important part in determining the style of production you are going to aim for. Are you going for a folky, airy sound with fairylike vocals and mandolin, or are you going for an in-your-face distortion-ridden art-metal extravaganza that would make Dream Theater blush?

Take recordings that you like the sound of and reference them before and during recording. Identify what you like about them, and try to incorporate those elements into your sound. There's no shame in using your influences in this way. The band whose album you are using as a reference probably referenced some other band's album when they were recording.

LISTEN FOR TECHNIQUES

When listening to other people's albums, try to get to the bottom of what it is you like about the recording. Is there a lot of reverb on the album? What other effects can you hear and are they important to the sound? Which instruments are prominent in the mix and how are they panned? Do the drums sound natural, like they would "in the room," or have they been heavily compressed and EQed to make them sound more "in your face" and aggressive? What about the vocals: where do they sit in the mix; are they close or far away? Keep asking questions and you may learn some valuable production techniques very cheaply!

› Conventional beginnings
The Beatles started out as a classic and rather conventional rock 'n' roll band before turning into the pioneering, experimental, genre-busting band everyone remembers them as today.

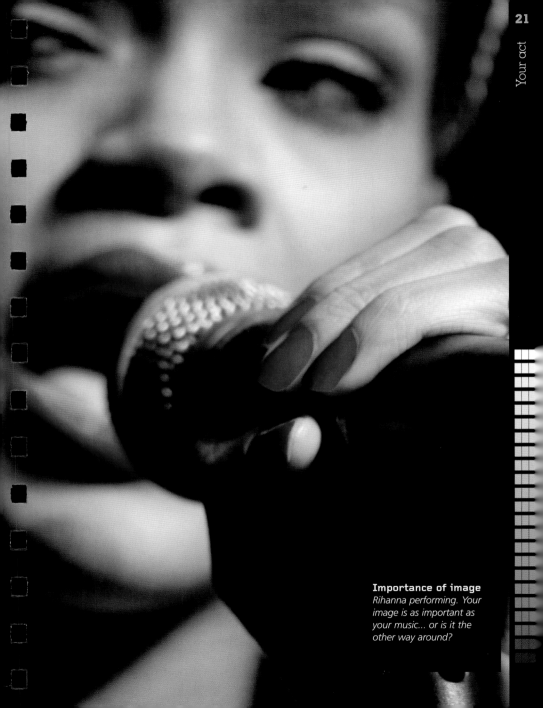

Importance of image
Rihanna performing. Your image is as important as your music... or is it the other way around?

Band name and image

Coming up with a good band name is an art in itself. You need to find a name that's original, catchy and—most importantly—not already taken.

Stage name

Whether you're a solo artist or in a group, sometimes you won't be happy with your birth name and you'll want something a bit more exciting. While you don't need to change your name legally, you might want to toy with the idea of a stage name. It's a lot more common than you might think.

A stage name might simply omit your last name (such as Madonna or Beyoncé) or be an alternative spelling of your name (such as James Marshall "Jimi" Hendrix). You could, however, consider completely reinventing your name like the following artists:

BIRTH NAME	STAGE NAME
Stefani Germanotta	Lady Gaga
Robert Zimmerman	Bob Dylan
Richard Starkey	Ringo Starr
Timothy Mosley	Timbaland

Doppelganger alert!

Naturally, you'll want your band or act to have a unique name. This is, however, not easy to achieve, as there are literally millions of unsigned acts all over the globe. Indeed, you might have already come across another unsigned act on the internet with "your" name. This is nothing to worry about at this stage; it only becomes an issue if either of you become so successful that anyone else using the same name could be accused of profiting from false association with

a crowd-pulling brand or identity. And if both of you become successful, you could hurt each other's reputation. The 1970s rock band Blue, for example, sued UK 1990s boy band Blue for allegedly damaging their career. Even song names aren't safe; the Red Hot Chili Peppers, for example, sued TV show "Californication" for identity theft. In short, make sure you don't clash with any successful names!

Image

If you think your act is "just about the music," you're fooling yourself. Fully-formed artists come as a stylistic whole that includes sonic identity, clothes, color schemes, favored geometric shapes, and cultural allegiances. The

CHOOSING A NAME

A good band name should:
- *Be easy to say, read, and spell*
- *Be short and memorable*
- *Have interesting or amusing double meanings that work with your music.*

A dubious band name might:
- *Be complicated or convoluted*
- *Be difficult to pronounce or spell*
- *Accidentally mean something inappropriate in another language*
- *Have obscure double meanings that don't correspond with your act.*

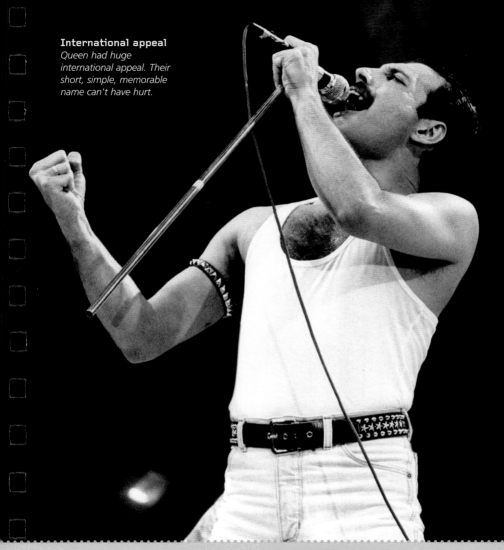

International appeal
Queen had huge international appeal. Their short, simple, memorable name can't have hurt.

CASE STUDY: QUEEN
It is hard to find a more successful choice of band name than "Queen." It's a short, memorable, everyday word that also connotes two very different, equally evocative ideas: royalty and homosexuality. Its lead singer Freddie Mercury, who came up with the name, was also a trained graphic illustrator and designed the famous Queen crest. He was so conscious of the presentation and marketing of his act that he also legally changed his name (from Farrokh Bulsara) around the time Queen was formed.

Controlled image
The White Stripes' masterful control over their image has increased their commercial success and popularity.

more all-encompassing your style is, the more convincing you will appear, and you might even be able to shake off that home-brew smell completely!

Visual design

Recognizable color schemes and shapes are a fantastic way to promote your music by attaching it to visual elements. The White Stripes are an extreme example, with the color red regularly juxtaposed with white in their artwork and onstage. Straight lines are obviously strong, but any simple shape—triangles, hexagons, ellipses, corn circles, letters of the alphabet—can provide a backdrop for more detailed visual creations such as cartoon figures, flowers, skulls, sofas, or cuddly toys. The manner of execution is key here, as it can convey a dramatically different lifestyle. Just imagine a mean skull intended for heavy-metal purposes drawn in pencil and colored in pastels...

The band's new clothes

Clothes are a minefield of connotation and lifestyle referencing. You need to be aware of how different clothes convey different ideas. Fashion changes far too quickly for any specific advice offered here to be useful. It is worth remembering, though, that your ability to adapt to changing fashions could make all the difference to your career. If you don't have a legion of fans who are attached to your current look, you could have nothing to lose and everything to gain by changing your wardrobe and overall style to whatever happens to be the "next big thing" at the time you're reading this.

Chapter 2

Equipment

 When it comes to recording, your choice of equipment will have a defining influence over your sound. You need to choose wisely, and you need to become familiar with the equipment that has shaped your favorite records. So before you start shopping, absorb some invaluable information!

Recording equipment basics

"If you don't have all the gear... better find some other way to improvise that dish." Frank Zappa

There's a vast and ever-growing amount of home recording equipment available, so purchasing the right equipment on a limited budget can seem impossibly daunting. This chapter covers the basic principles of recording and the gear involved.

The main players

When you record, you aim to capture vibrating air (sound) and turn it into a hard disk file so it can be burnt to CD or turned into an MP3 for internet distribution. A sound source is defined as anything that makes air vibrate at audible frequencies: a French horn, a didgeridoo, a human voice, a guitar amplifier. The sound source is captured using a microphone, a

Frank Zappa
Frank Zappa likened the recording process to cooking. Even if you don't have a lot of money and good equipment, you can still get a good result...

ESSENTIAL INGREDIENTS FOR RECORDING

Outboard equipment, cables, and soundproofing—*the hardware you'll use in the recording process and how you connect it up. You'll*
also need to consider soundproofing and acoustic treatment. See pages 30–31 and 36–37.

Microphones—*these turn sound waves (from voices or instruments) into electrical signals. See pages 40–51.*

Pre-amplifiers—*these fine-tune the sound from your mic, by making it louder or "coloring" it in some way, for example. See pages 52–53.*

Compressors—*these level out the dynamic range of a recording (making*

device capable of turning sound into electricity. From there, the electrical signal goes into a DAW (digital audio workstation)—a computer with recording software on it. This saves the electrical signal as a file that can be played back—your "track." In order to hear what you're doing, you need monitor speakers (or monitors) and headphones. Processors and effects allow you to manipulate the recorded sound in practical and playful ways, both while you're recording and afterward during "mixing."

The hidden players

Different pieces of the above equipment operate at different voltages or nominal levels, and amplifiers are needed to convert electrical signals from one level to another. The most important is the preamplifier, a device that boosts the signal of a microphone from "microphone level" to "line level" so it can be recorded.

Turning an electrical signal into computer code and back requires designated equipment called converters. An electrical signal is known as analog; a computer code signal is known as digital.

DEDICATION TO THE CAUSE

As you might be aware, many operations (such as conversion and preamplification) can be performed by integrated, mass-produced, one-size-fits-all components in your computer or, say, a USB microphone. However, using a well-marketed, all-in-one solution for your recording can result in a cheap-sounding and distinctly amateurish final product. A classic home recordist's mistake is to assume that shoddily recorded sound can be fixed with software—it can't. A professional sound requires an appreciation of the signal chain (see page 32), and attention to its every stage. Only dedicated equipment can help you achieve this.

This chapter will discuss each engineering concept in turn, and suggest a range of dedicated (purpose-built) gear for performing each task.

quiet bits louder and loud bits quieter), and can provide other effects. See pages 58–63.

Equalization—*EQ can filter out frequencies and manipulate them to correct problems in the recording. See pages 64–69.*

Interfaces and converters—*these are part of the process of turning an analog signal into a digital output and vice versa. See pages 72–77.*

Digital audio workstations—*DAWs provide a means of*

recording and manipulating multiple tracks. See pages 78–81.

Monitors—*these are high-quality speakers (not computer screens!) designed for tracking and mixing music. See pages 82–87.*

Outboard equipment

There are many stages in the recording signal chain (see page 32), and each one is traditionally associated with a particular piece of outboard gear—stand-alone hardware dedicated to a specific task. You'll still need the computer to store your sound as hard disk files, but other duties can be performed externally.

Most audio processing equipment consists of electronic circuitry housed in a metal box, the obvious exceptions being microphones and monitor speakers. On the front panel, rotary controls, switches, and meters allow the user to change parameters, while keeping an eye on signal levels. At the rear end, you'll find various different sockets, most importantly for input and output. These are self-explanatory; a signal enters the unit through the input socket and the processed signal exits via the output.

Rack-mounted gear
A typical studio rack, complete with EQs, compressors, and preamps. Rack-mounted gear doesn't just make for a better-equipped studio, it also looks stylish!

> **Hooking up**
Outboard equipment needs to be hooked up correctly, and some pieces of gear have sockets on the front as well as the rear panel to facilitate this. This makes it very easy to adapt your signal chain to your recording needs.

In the studio

A view inside a recording studio, with rack-mounted outboard equipment visible to the right of the picture.

› Outboard dimensions

The dimensions of most outboard audio equipment allow them to be screw-mounted into standard studio racks. This illustration shows a typical standardized system for mounting equipment.

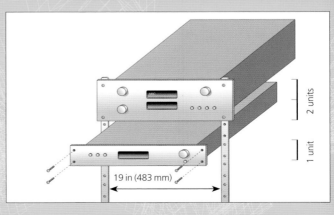

2 units

1 unit

19 in (483 mm)

The signal chain

As you record your music, the original sound passes through many permutations and devices before it is committed to hard disk, and even more before it can be heard through speakers.

1 Sound: Your studio environment is where all your sound, from guitars to speakers, is going to happen. The problem is, sound reflects, and as it reflects, it colors and pollutes the original sound—whether you're recording or monitoring. Some basic acoustic treatment, from hanging quilts to purpose-built bass traps, will minimize reflections and help insulate the room. Also, any sound source should be positioned carefully before recording begins.

2 Microphones: Unless you intend to use samples, MIDI instruments, and synths for your entire album, you're going to have to record your playing and singing through some kind of microphone.

3 Preamplification: Microphone output signals are tiny, so they need to be amplified from microphone level to line level before they can be processed and recorded. Preamps provide signal amplification as well as character and color.

4 Processing your signal: Your recorded track will probably need some "ironing out"—dynamic range control, tweaking the timbre, getting rid of background noise… compressors and equalizers polish your signal off, replacing the original signal with a superior version. This can take place when recording (as shown), mixing, or even mastering— it's never too late to process!

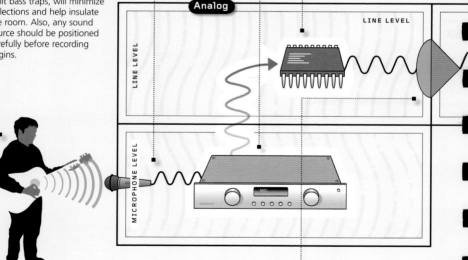

5 Turning your electrical signal into computer code: Unless you're using a tape machine, you'll be recording your opus onto a hard disk, so an A/D converter will have to convert the signal from analog to digital.

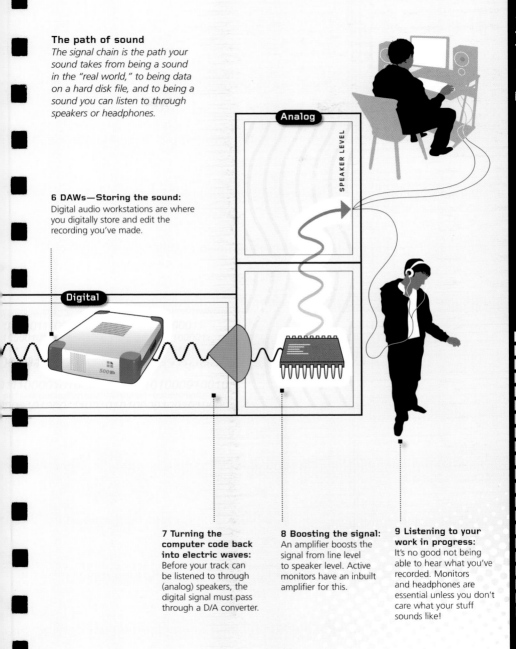

The path of sound

The signal chain is the path your sound takes from being a sound in the "real world," to being data on a hard disk file, and to being a sound you can listen to through speakers or headphones.

Analog

SPEAKER LEVEL

6 DAWs—Storing the sound:
Digital audio workstations are where you digitally store and edit the recording you've made.

Digital

500gb

7 Turning the computer code back into electric waves:
Before your track can be listened to through (analog) speakers, the digital signal must pass through a D/A converter.

8 Boosting the signal:
An amplifier boosts the signal from line level to speaker level. Active monitors have an inbuilt amplifier for this.

9 Listening to your work in progress:
It's no good not being able to hear what you've recorded. Monitors and headphones are essential unless you don't care what your stuff sounds like!

The decibel

Before you start thinking about equipment, it's important to become familiar with the most important measurement in audio: the decibel (dB).

A decibel is not a unit, but simply a measurement of a level of power (sound pressure, voltage, etc). A reference point is chosen—such as the threshold of human hearing—against which the measured power will be held up against—in this case, sound pressure. If it's higher (a car driving past your house), you have a positive number of decibels; if it's lower (a mouse running past your house), a negative number.

Decibels in music production

Decibels are used to measure all sorts of things, including sound pressure, absolute and relative power levels, noise levels, and gain staging (difference in output between pieces of equipment). Here's a selection of decibel units you'll need to know:

> **dB:** Sound pressure relative to the threshold of human hearing. See "How loud is it?" opposite.

> **dB**: This isn't a typo—dB can also refer to relative increases in power and voltage in pieces of equipment (preamp gain, for example, would be measured like this).

> **dBu** (unloaded): Voltage relative to 0.7745 V rms. Audio signal levels are usually measured in this unit. See "Nominal levels and gain staging" below.

> **dBFS** (full scale): Wave amplitudes of a soundcard measured relative to its clipping point (see page 128). If you ever come across this unit, just make sure you stay below zero, or everything will start distorting horribly!

NOMINAL LEVELS AND GAIN STAGING

Engineers distinguish three operating levels for various pieces of recording equipment. They are measured in dBu, which refers to the output voltage.

Mic level (or low level):
-infinity to -20 dBu: Microphones, guitar pickups.

Line level (or medium level):
-20 dBu to +30 dBu: Preamps, keyboards, effects processors, consoles.

Speaker level (or high level):
+30 dBu upward: Guitar amps, speakers, monitors.

HOW LOUD IS IT?

You may have come across decibels as a way of measuring sound pressure (or loudness):

- **-Infinity:** *Silence*
- **-20 dB:** *A spider crawling across a wall*
- **0 dB:** *The threshold of human hearing*
- **15–20 dB:** *A whisper*
- **50–60 dB:** *Normal conversation*
- **70–90 dB:** *Shouting*
- **120 dB:** *A rock concert or an airplane taking off*
- **130 dB:** *Pain threshold*
- **150 dB:** *A space shuttle launching beside an erupting volcano!*

▶ TOP TIP

When connecting audio equipment, be aware of the levels at either end of the cable. Do they match up? Will anything overload? Some preamps, for instance, provide separate input sockets for keyboards (often labeled "instrument") and microphones. A microphone plugged into the instrument socket will barely register, and an electric piano plugged into the mic socket will overload the preamp's circuit. Try to be aware of the nominal level you're working with.

Audio cables and sockets

Hooking up your equipment is an art in itself, and professional studios often take weeks to get wired up. You're aware of gain staging (see page 34); now make sure you know which cables to use on which sockets.

Analog

TS
(Tip, sleeve/unbalanced)
TS is the simplest audio cable. It transports an electrical signal across two wires. These inexpensive cables are ideal provided they're short; longer cables can generate considerable self-noise.

TS cable

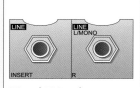

TS and TRS sockets

TRS
(Tip, ring, sleeve/balanced)
TRS is essentially the same as TS, but the extra wire allows for any hum created by the cable to be canceled. Remember that this only works if the sockets being used are balanced as well.

TRS socket
TS and TRS cables share the same type of socket (see above), but a TRS socket is labeled "Balanced."

TRS cable

XLR
(Center, left, right/balanced)
The XLR is a three-wire cable like the TRS with the same noise-cancelation properties, but with different connectors. Most microphones have XLR outputs.

XLR cable

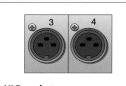

XLR socket

Combo jack
A combo jack is a neat socket that accepts both TRS and XLR cables.

Combo jack

Tech talk

MIDI cable

A MIDI cable doesn't transmit sound, digital, or analog. It transmits MIDI (Music Instrument Digital Interface) information, a kind of language that lets instruments and DAWs (see page 76) communicate. An in-depth discussion of MIDI is beyond the scope of this book, but it's a useful tool thanks to its clocking and synchronization facilities.

A MIDI cable

Digital

Coaxial

A copper wire transmits digital signals in pulses of electricity. This cable is ideal for sending digital signals from one piece of digital gear straight to another without having to convert the signal.

Coaxial cable

Coaxial socket

Optical

Instead of electricity, a beam of pulsating light is sent through the cable. Unlike with coaxial cables, the signal doesn't degrade over the distance of the cable, which makes it superior (but more expensive).

Optical cable

Optical socket

Positioning, acoustic treatment, and soundproofing

Your home studio is the space where you listen to speakers and record instruments—make sure you can monitor clearly, and that your room doesn't sound like a shoebox.

reflections. A duvet is a good start, and acoustic foam or even egg cartons will help absorb sound and break up the flatness of the original surface to help eliminate reflections.

Absorbing material

Sound in an "untreated" studio will reflect off flat surfaces as it fills the room and color your original sound, making your recording sound boxy and modulated and your speakers unclear. Acoustic treatment in your room will minimize reflections and create a space where you can record a purer sound and hear your speakers more clearly.

Covering flat surfaces such as walls is the first step to minimizing

Soundproofing

If you want to record drums until four in the morning, you'll need to think of ways of not waking up the neighbors! Soundproofing is all about getting your studio as well-insulated as possible. If you live in a flat, it's a good idea to keep any loud, resonant objects floating rather than on the floor: monitors and guitar amps should rest on thick absorbent material (such as rockwool or neoprene slabs). Remember that wooden floors are extremely resonant, so a covering of carpet will help.

SOUNDPROOFING SOLUTIONS

Universal Acoustics Jupiter Wedge (budget): *These wedges of absorbent foam can be used as guitar amp stands, or adhered to the wall to absorb reflections.*

Acousti Pro Bass Master Wedge (mid-price): *This bass trap absorbs bass frequencies specifically,*

and is mounted to a top corner of your room.

SE Electronics Reflexion Filter Portable Vocal Booth (expensive): *This ingenious device is mounted on your microphone stand, protecting the microphone from reflections. Excellent as a last resort in a boomy or boxy room.*

China cones acoustic decoupler (expensive): *These little ceramic cones act as stands to speakers or audio equipment, and isolate the vibrations inside the equipment from the surface they are resting on. Diminutive in size, they are surprisingly effective, and look very elegant.*

MONITOR POSITIONING

Every monitoring situation is different, but as a general rule you should try to form an equilateral triangle when you position your speakers, with the distance between each monitor and the listening position being equal.

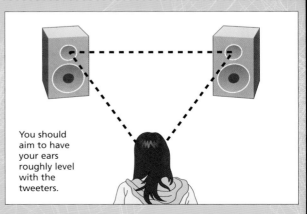

You should aim to have your ears roughly level with the tweeters.

● **SEE ALSO** *The signal chain* **32** *Polar patterns* **42**

How do microphones work?

Microphones transduce (change) sound into electrical energy, and they do so in two stages.

1 Turning vibrating air into vibrating metal: the diaphragm

An ultra-thin suspended diaphragm in the microphone capsule vibrates in response to incoming sound waves. (Imagine a miniature round sail flapping backward and forward in temperamental winds, then speed it up.) The diaphragm is either made of metal itself or is coupled to a vibrating element made of metal. It's made of metal because metal conducts electricity and air doesn't, and an electrical signal can only be extracted from a material that's conductive.

How the diaphragm is suspended and housed in the microphone determines how well it can pick up incoming sound from different directions—this is called its *pickup* or *polar pattern* (see page 42).

2 Turning vibrating metal into an electrical signal: transduction

So now the piece of metal is fluttering in the sonic wind… but this fluttering needs to be turned into electricity. What's needed is some kind of force-field that can extract electrical "meaning" from the moving conductor. Different mics use different fields and electronic components to achieve this. The method used determines the microphone type (see page 46).

> **› How a microphone works**
>
> This cutaway shows the component parts of a typical diaphragm microphone.

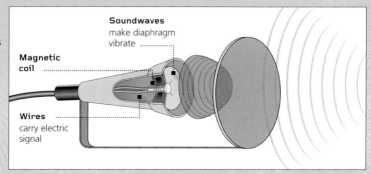

Soundwaves make diaphragm vibrate

Magnetic coil

Wires carry electric signal

Large, medium, or small

Large diaphragms— ¾ in (18 mm) or larger—are very sensitive, but also add a fair bit of coloration to your sound. They are traditionally used for a "big" sound, particularly on vocals. Small diaphragms, on the other hand, are lighter and faster, and so capture transients and high frequencies better, adding brightness and definition to the sound. These diaphragms are generally considered to be ⅝ in (15 mm) or smaller. A happy medium between small and large is the medium-sized diaphragm, which exhibits a combination of both the "big" and the "clear" characteristics.

PROTECTING YOUR MICROPHONE

Diaphragms are sensitive little things. Shaking stands and flowing air (displaced air from a heavy-footed drummer's kick drum, for example, or a singer breathing directly into the microphone) can force the diaphragm to vibrate heavily, resulting in unwanted noise on your recording. To stop unwanted airflow, mesh or foam "windscreens" are provided with most microphones. In addition, you can use pop shields when recording studio vocals to avoid "popping" on consonants with explosive airflow (such as "p," "b," "k," "h," and "t"). Shock mounts suspend a microphone inside a metal frame so that it effectively floats when the mic stand is knocked or shaken.

Polar patterns

A pickup, or polar, pattern describes how well a microphone's diaphragm responds to sound depending on the angle at which sound approaches it.

Depending on the range of directions from which a microphone can faithfully capture sound, its polar pattern is classified as "unidirectional," "bidirectional," or "omnidirectional."

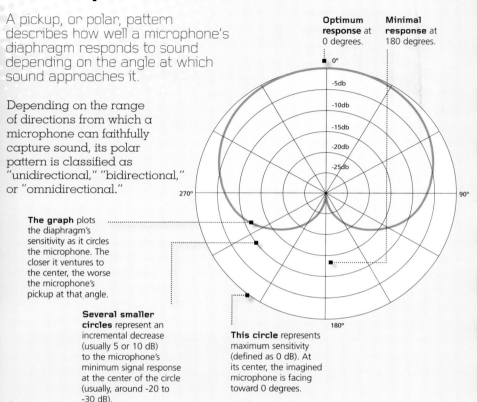

Optimum response at 0 degrees.

Minimal response at 180 degrees.

The graph plots the diaphragm's sensitivity as it circles the microphone. The closer it ventures to the center, the worse the microphone's pickup at that angle.

Several smaller circles represent an incremental decrease (usually 5 or 10 dB) to the microphone's minimum signal response at the center of the circle (usually, around -20 to -30 dB).

This circle represents maximum sensitivity (defined as 0 dB). At its center, the imagined microphone is facing toward 0 degrees.

TIME WARP!
Recording Glenn Gould —a leakage nightmare
Glenn Gould (1932–1982) was a renowned classical pianist whose fresh, stripped-down interpretations of J.S. Bach's works singlehandedly blew the cobwebs off this great composer. His first and defining record, a rendition of Bach's "Goldberg Variations" (1955, Columbia), was an overnight sensation. The problem the sound engineer faced when recording Gould was that he insisted on humming along quite loudly while he was playing.

A combination of careful microphone choice and placement and not-so-subtle EQ was the only answer. Even then, you could still hear him.

‹ Bach's influence
JS Bach's (1685–1750) influence reaches as far as jazz, art-metal, and mainstream pop.

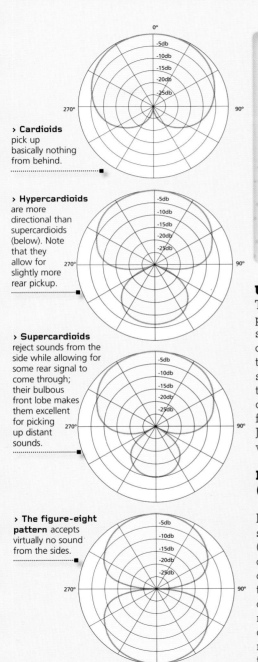

> **Cardioids** pick up basically nothing from behind.

> **Hypercardioids** are more directional than supercardioids (below). Note that they allow for slightly more rear pickup.

> **Supercardioids** reject sounds from the side while allowing for some rear signal to come through; their bulbous front lobe makes them excellent for picking up distant sounds.

> **The figure-eight pattern** accepts virtually no sound from the sides.

Unidirectional patterns

The cardioid is *the* classic polar pattern. It gets its name from its supposed heart shape—think cardiac arrest—though in Germany it is thought to have more of a kidney shape! This pattern allows for sound to be captured faithfully from one direction only. This makes it popular for preventing leakage (see above). Just make sure your mic is facing what you want to record.

Bidirectional (figure-eight) patterns

Figure-eight patterns are the signature of the ribbon microphone (see page 49). The metal ribbon can receive sounds from the two directions its flat sides are exposed to. As long as there is no sound coming from behind, a figure-eight microphone will behave much like a cardioid one. It can also be used to record two instruments or more at the same time, placed inside a small brass ensemble for example.

Omnidirectional patterns

Omnidirectional microphones (known as omnis) are built to pick up sound from any direction equally well. They have an even frequency response and are considered to be the most true-to-life microphones. They are also less vulnerable to external airflow. Their only downside is that they are prone to leakage, for obvious reasons.

Polar patterns across the frequency spectrum

It's very important to note that polar patterns change across the frequency spectrum. In other words, their shape at 100 Hz is usually quite different from that at 15 kHz. This is often illustrated on one diagram with several, differently colored parts.

Frequency response

Frequency response diagrams illustrate how accurately a transducer (a microphone or loudspeaker) converts the frequency spectrum of the input signal (sound, electricity). You will encounter these when properties of microphones and monitors are being discussed. "Off-axis frequency response" refers to the response off the main axis of the object in question.

Summary

Knowing a microphone's polar pattern is essential to using it correctly. Be aware of your mic's minumum and maximum sensitivity angles and position it accordingly.

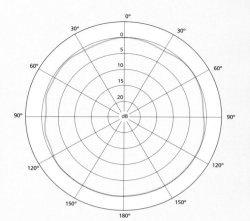

Omnidirectional response
These mics have a near-perfect circular pickup graph.

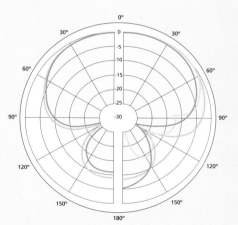

Off-axis response
In the pattern for the supercardioid microphone shown above, response off the axis (known as off-axis response) varies across the frequency spectrum, indicated in different colors. This will affect your recorded sound if your microphone isn't well placed.

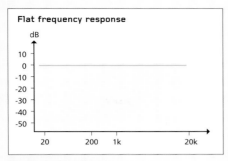

Flat frequency response

The ideal microphone

In an ideal world, every frequency your microphone picked up would be transduced equally. This utopian microphone would have a flat frequency response, as shown in the graph above.

THE SM57

The frequency response of the SM57 (see below) is relatively poor around 60 Hz and gradually ascends and stabilizes around 0 dB at 150 Hz. This means that any bassy, rumbling sounds recorded won't shine through—definitely a bad idea if you're miking a bass guitar amp, but fantastic if you're miking up a nearby, bass-light instrument and want to avoid bass guitar bleed. The frequency response subsequently stays pretty much flat until about 4 kHz, and from there it gradually ascends to peak at around 7.5 kHz. This will definitely add some presence and brightness to the mic's output, which is desirable in some situations.

So what instrument would be good for this mic? Well, almost anything! A light bass response lends clarity to the sound, and that high-end boost brightens it. Voice, electric guitar, drums (apart from the kick, perhaps), all are welcome…

> **Shure SM57 frequency response**
Notice the relatively flat frequency response in the middle of the spectrum. The "bumps" on either side give the SM57 its distinct character.

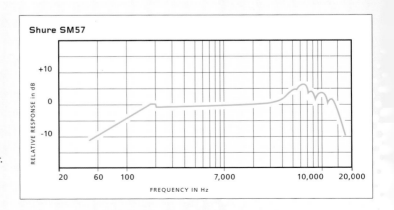

Shure SM57

▶ **SEE ALSO** *Polar patterns* **42** *Recording basics* **102**

Microphone types

The mic you choose will depend on its ruggedness, reliability, character, size, and price. To a recording musician, there are three mic types of interest: dynamic, condenser, and ribbon.

Shure SM57

Dynamic microphones

A dynamic mic works just like a dynamo, hence the name: a coil of wire moving inside a magnetic field induces an electrical current in the wire. In the case of a dynamic microphone, the coil is mounted around a permanent magnet and attached to a sound-sensitive diaphragm. When the diaphragm vibrates, the coil has room to do so too. This induces an electrical current in the wire, which results in an electrical representation of the sound wave that originally struck the diaphragm. This electrical representation can then be amplified and manipulated farther along the signal chain (see page 32).

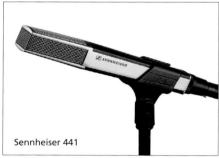

Sennheiser 441

AKG D112

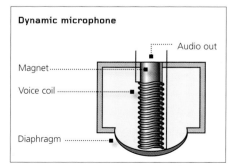

Dynamic microphone

Audio out

Magnet

Voice coil

Diaphragm

Pros	Cons
• Rugged—excellent for live performance • Colorful sound • Inexpensive • Insensitive to humidity or heat • Can handle high SPLs • Don't need power	• Generally not "true-to-life" compared with condenser mics

Mics for live use

Chris Martin of Coldplay performing. You need to consider the properties of microphones for live performances just as you would for recording.

>> Tech talk

Induction

The dynamo principle is a simple, reliable method of transducing mechanical movement into electricity, and vice versa. If you move a wire coil in a magnetic field, you get a current across that wire—simple! So simple in fact that it can be found in many microphones, and all loudspeakers and guitar pickups. In fact some microphones, such as those found in walkie-talkies and intercoms, can be used as speakers because the designs are so similar. Whatever the implementation, induction is a reliable method of transduction without which music equipment would be less predictable, more expensive, and more confusing.

Condenser (or capacitor) microphones

The condenser microphone is named after its main electrical component, the capacitor or condenser. This consists of two metal "plates" separated by a gap of air. When a bias voltage is applied to the capacitor, the plates are charged, generating an electrostatic field. One of these plates is the diaphragm, one that is about a twentieth of the weight of a dynamic mic's diaphragm, making it faster and more responsive. When it vibrates, the gap between the plates fluctuates, which in turn alters the voltage across the plates. This voltage is an electrical representation of the diaphragm's vibrations. The resulting current, however, is tiny, so an inbuilt amplifier reduces impedance and boosts the signal.

Audio Technica 4033a

AKG 451

JARGON BUSTER

Transients

Transients are specific frequencies in a sound wave that occur for a very brief time, usually in the initial sharp attack of a sound. Transient-rich instruments are ones that are plucked, struck, or hit: acoustic guitars, pianos, drums, percussion, tap-dancing. Heavy diaphragms take too long to respond to these fleeting attack sounds, so use small-diaphragm condenser or ribbon microphones to capture their essential percussive qualities.

Condenser microphone

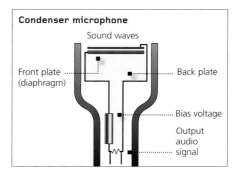

Sound waves

Front plate (diaphragm) · · · · · · · · Back plate

· · · · · · · · Bias voltage

· · · · · · · · Output audio signal

▲ Pros	● Cons
• Sensitive, fast-responding	• Expensive
• Transparent, true-to-life	• Sensitive to humidity and heat
• Good transient response and dynamic range	• Fragile
	• Need power

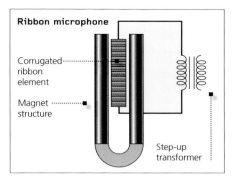

Ribbon microphone

Corrugated ribbon element

Magnet structure

Step-up transformer

Ribbon microphones

Ribbon microphones are a type of dynamic microphone. A permanent magnet still functions as the force field, but instead of a metal coil winding around it, a very fine corrugated ribbon made of metal is suspended in a gap inside the magnet. As it vibrates, a voltage across the ribbon is induced by the magnetic field.

Fragile, old-fashioned, and delicate

The ribbons in old microphones were so sensitive that sneezing on them (even through the microphone's protective mesh) actually broke them! Luckily, ribbon microphones are now more robust, though they remain the most vulnerable microphones in use. Having said that, they do have excellent transient response (see opposite) and sound beautiful.

PHANTOM OF THE STUDIO

Condenser mics require power for both bias voltage and amplification. A console can sneakily introduce it via a regular XLR audio cable, and only condenser mics can "tell" it's even there. Appropriately, it's called "phantom power." Contrary to popular myth, dynamic and ribbon microphones can't be damaged by phantom power unless the cabling between devices is faulty. All the same, it's a good idea to avoid switching phantom power on when a ribbon mic is at the receiving end. Most tube condenser microphones, incidentally, can't be phantom-powered, and require a dedicated power supply with special cabling.

Pros	Cons
• Good sonic reproduction	• Expensive
• Gorgeous, rounded sound	• Very fragile
	• Unsuitable for live use
	• Too "dark" for some tastes

Microphone buyer's guide

A selection of microphones of different types to suit all budgets, with advice on their strengths, weaknesses, and potential uses.

Shure SM57
- **Budget dynamic**
- **Cardioid**

The SM57 is the ultimate microphone—period. It can be used on just about any source successfully, it's inexpensive, and even the most exclusive recording studio will have at least four of them in their mic locker. The only downside is that there are quite a few counterfeit SM57s floating around on the secondhand market, so be careful. Check out the SM58, too, which is an excellent vocal mic that has been used to record Bono and Bryan Adams, among others.

• Use the SM57 on: Anything! It's not the ideal mic for acoustic guitar and piano, but you should try it on everything, especially snare drum and guitar amp, where it's unbeatable.

AKG D112
- **Budget dynamic**
- **Cardioid**

The AKG D112 is the industry-standard kick drum mic. It has exceptional SPL handling (up to 160 dB) and a presence rise at 4kHz that helps a kick sound cut through a mix. Some engineers prefer the original AKG D12; look out for that one secondhand.
• Use the D112 on: Kick drum, bass guitar amp, trombone.

Sennheiser 441
- **Mid-priced dynamic**
- **Supercardioid**

The Sennheiser 441 might fall into the mid-priced category, but for a dynamic mic it's about as pricey and esoteric as it gets. Sennheiser designed the 441 to combine the best features of condenser and dynamic microphones: true-to-life accuracy and superior SPL handling and ruggedness, respectively.
• Use the 441 on: Vocals, brass instruments, guitar amp, toms. Combine with a high quality preamp for a very "hi-fi," crystalline sound without hyped high-frequency response.

ShinyBox 46MX
- **Budget ribbon**
- **Figure-eight**

There was a time not so long ago when you had to fork out serious money for a good ribbon mic. But times have changed, thanks partly to an influx of relatively inexpensive components from China. ShinyBox is Jon Ulrigg who carefully selects components and

assembles and fine-tunes each microphone himself. The ShinyBox 46MX is a real giant-killer!
• *Use the 46MX on: Overheads, piano, acoustic guitar.*

Beyer M160
• **Mid-priced ribbon**
• **Hypercardioid**

Not your typical ribbon microphone, the Beyer M160 uses two aluminum ribbons that are only .0002 in apart to produce a robust, hypercardioid mic. If you're planning on recording drums, you won't find a warmer, punchier pair of overheads than two M160s.
• *Use the M160 on: Overheads, guitar amps, occasional vocals.*

AKG 451
• **Budget SDC (secondhand)**
• **Cardioid**

The 451 is a sparkly, bright condenser mic, ideal for capturing sources that are rich in transients. A very useful, high-quality mic that doesn't always get the praise it deserves.
• *Use the 451 on: Hi-hats, acoustic guitar, tambourine.*

Josephson C42
• **Mid-priced SDC**
• **Cardioid**

Josephson make condenser mics exclusively and all of their microphones are of the very highest quality, which makes the affordability of the excellent C42 all the more amazing.
• *Use the C42 on: Acoustic guitar, piano, overheads, occasional vocals…*
try it on any acoustic instrument.

Audio Technica 4033a
• **Budget LDC**
• **Cardioid**

Some people will tell you that in order to record a big, million-dollar vocal sound you need an expensive microphone with an exclusive badge on the front. You will be pleased to hear that those people are wrong: the Audio Technica 4033a is a fantastic vocal microphone with a big sound and a rich, airy top end.
• *Use the 4033 on: Vocals, acoustic guitar.*

Brauner VMX
• **Expensive LDC**
• **Continuously variable polar pattern**

Dirk Brauner's Frankfurt-based company makes astonishing large-diaphragm condenser mics that can rival those of Neumann and Gefell. The Brauner VMX boasts an infinitely variable polar pattern and a characterful frequency response with a smooth top end and a slightly accentuated low–mid bottom end.
• *Use the VMX on: Vocals, strings, double bass.*

Neumann U47
• **Fantasy island LDC**
• **Omnidirectional and cardioid**

The Neumann U47 (in particular, the original, tube U47) is probably the most sought-after microphone in the world alongside the Ela M 251, AKG C12, and RCA DX77. It is famous for imbuing recordings with a warm, rich, full sound. As well as being Sir George Martin's favorite microphone, it is said that at one time Frank Sinatra refused to sing into anything else!

Preamplifiers

Preamps are critical to your signal chain, but they're more than mere signal carriers. They can offer elegant distortion, a warm analog feel, punchy drive, or crisp, transparent amplification—you choose. This is the place to fine-tune your mic sound.

Why amplify?

Preamps are born of necessity. Output voltages of microphones are too small for recording equipment to process and preamps amplify these tiny voltages by a factor of up to a million. This gain boost brings the input signal from microphone level to line level (see page 34). Two methods of amplification are used in preamps: tubes and transistors (see page 54). A preamp's character is largely determined by these components.

Preamps are all around

If you think you've never seen a preamp in your life, think again. If you've ever recorded music with a microphone or electric guitar, you've inadvertently used one. Stand-alone recorders, computer soundcards, consoles, and even USB microphones all have integrated preamps to boost the microphone signal. The quality of your preamps largely determines the pedigree of your recording system. If you've ever adjusted the trim on a recording system, you've been playing with the preamp's gain, but as you're serious about recording, those run-of-the-mill built-in preamps just aren't going to cut it anymore. Stand-alone, dedicated preamps offer not just a superior, more faithful amplification, but also the possibility of "seasoning" the sound with their own individual character. Different preamps "suit" different mics.

GAIN CONTROL

Dedicated preamplifiers and outboard channel strips offer several advantages over lesser, built-in amplifiers:

1. Character: *All preamps have their own tone color, feel, and drive, and can add a whole new layer of interest to your sound.*

2. Choice: *You choose the preamp that you think will fit your music (see Buyers' guide, page 56).*

3. Flexibility: *Many preamps come with a whole host of features, from different impedance and circuitry options to three-band EQ!*

▶ **TOP TIP**

A high-end mixing console will have excellent preamplification circuitry on every single one of its channels.

Methods of amplification

All analog equipment is biased toward one of two amplification methods: transistors ("solid-state") or vacuum tubes. Tubes have been around since 1907 and transistors were invented 40 years later. In most fields of engineering, tubes are considered obsolete; in music production, however, they're almost fetishized for their gently distorted, "warm" sound. Transistors are considered more "clean" and transparent.

Not just for microphones

Most preamps are designed to amplify microphones. But a preamp's ability to make a signal more rounded, colorful, or interesting is begging to be abused. Preamps, therefore, are inserted all over the signal chain. An electro-pop synth whizz-kid, for example, might want her synth mixes to have a more "analog" (i.e. warm, fuzzy, and tube-y) feel to them, so she would perhaps record some of her synth parts through a tube preamp, or even run her entire mix through it. Some electronic synths even provide an inbuilt tube preamp simply for warming up the sound...

‹ Transistor
Transistors require no warming up, and are very rugged. They are also considerably smaller than tubes.

‹ Tube
The metal components in a tube gradually heat up after being switched on, and reach an optimum operation temperature after about 30 minutes, so always allow your tube equipment to heat up. Over time, the filament that creates the heat will burn out, at which point the tube needs replacing.

DIRECT INJECTION

Direct injection, or DI, is usually used as a method of converting a high-impedance line level signal to a mic level signal. Effectively, this means you are able to plug an electric guitar or bass directly into a DI box and you will end up with a usable signal that can be routed directly to

your preamp or mixer. DI was famously used in 1967 to record Paul McCartney's bass on the Beatles' "Sgt. Pepper's Lonely Hearts Club Band" and, if you are planning to record bass guitar, or you intend to record a dry electric guitar signal and apply ITB amp modeling, then a DI of some sort is essential.

›Hendrix's sound
Jimi Hendrix's guitar sound is the epitome of warm, fuzzy amplification. The amplifiers in his Marshall stacks used tubes.

DRIVE IT!

Tubes can be "overdriven" by feeding them slightly more voltage than they are designed to handle, which creates a warm, rich harmonic saturation and distortion (often known as "fuzz"). After being discovered and popularized using damaged guitar amps, manufacturers soon found themselves building amps with an inbuilt overdrive facility.

Preamp and channel strip buyer's guide

A selection of preamps and channel strips to suit all budgets.

Studio Projects VTB-1
- **Budget**
- **Single channel mic pre**

The Studio Projects VTB-1 is an innovative pre that allows you to blend solid-state and tube characteristics to taste and also functions as a very effective instrument amplifier, complete with a "Hi-Z" input for DI. The tube stage uses a "starved plate" design that some users might find a little rough around the edges (though guitarists will love it!), but thankfully the tube stage can be bypassed, leaving you with discrete class-A/B solid-state excellence.

ART Pro Channel
- **Budget**
- **Mono channel strip**

The ART Pro Channel is a tremendous bang-for-your-buck channel strip incorporating a tube mic pre, a switchable tube/opto compressor, and a tube EQ. Capable of clean or warm pre-amplification and aggressive compression, the unit features insert points before and after the compressor stage, making it a versatile tool for mixing as well as tracking. The only downside is that the pro channel isn't a particularly impressive tool for DI instrument tracking.

DAV BG1
- **Mid-priced**
- **Dual channel mic pre**

The DAV BG1 is a truly high-end piece of equipment that is modestly priced. DAV are a small company based in Twickenham, England, and they're famous for reproducing some of the classic equipment used in Decca studios. If you're looking for a preamp that doubles as a DI, look elsewhere. But if you want a low noise, low distortion "big" sounding pre, check this out—you might find yourself preferring it to pres that cost three times as much.

Great River MP500
- **Mid-priced**
- **Single channel mic pre**

Great River make an absolute classic of a preamp, the MP-2NV, which is a favorite of recording engineers the world over because of its Neve-like, big, warm 1970s sound. The only problem is that the MP-2NV is an expensive piece of equipment, beyond the means of the average home user. If you own a 500-series rack, however, you're in luck because the MP500 brings that same, huge sound to a compact,

ART Pro Channel

affordable unit. An added bonus is its superb performance as a DI.

Sytek MPX-4Aii
- **Mid-priced**
- **Four-channel mic pre**

If you want the quality of an API or SSL preamp and you don't want to "pay for the label," the MPX-4Aii is worth checking out. Sytek are a Chicago-based company who are well known in the recording industry and (sadly) less well known by the typical home recordist. The four channels of preamplification on offer here are of the class-A, solid-state, clean, and transparent variety. If you want color, these pres might not be for you, but for those who value fidelity, uncompromising clarity, and a superb reproduction of transient-rich sources like drums, the MPX-4Aii is as good as anything.

Crane Song Flamingo
- **Expensive**
- **Dual channel mic pre**

Crane Song cater for the top end of the market and the Flamingo is definitely hoping to compete in the "best money-no-object preamp" category. It has some unusual design features such as a "warm" switch that can, well,

Neve 1073

warm up the sound. If you could only own one preamp, the Flamingo would be ideal.

Avalon 737sp
- **Expensive**
- **Mono channel strip**

A list of hit-record vocals that have been recorded through the 737 would be very, very long, which is a testament to the phenomenal success of this channel strip. The unit looks fantastic and features a class-A tube preamp, smooth opto compressor, and a superb, discrete class-A equalizer. As a bass guitar DI it's hard to beat, and if you want a crystalline, airy vocal sound the 737 would be a good choice. After all, if it's good enough for Christina Aguilera…

Universal Audio 610
- **Expensive**
- **Mono channel strip**

The preamp and EQ on the Avalon are world-beaters;

the compressor section is merely very good. What if you want a channel strip that incorporates a world-beating pre and compressor? The UA 610 includes a "leveling amplifier"-type compressor that uses the T4 optical circuitry found in the legendary LA-2A Teletronix compressor. Combine that with a real "proven classic" pre and a superb DI and you have a serious recording tool.

Neve 1073
- **Fantasy island**
- **Mic pre**

The Neve 1073 is still the pre to end all pres, more than 30 years after its introduction, and the original modules are increasingly hard to come by. It's not the fastest, cleanest preamp in the universe, but that's not the point. The 1073 imparts the quintessential Neve sound, one that's warm, punchy, and massive.

Compression

Understanding the fundamentals of compression is essential if you want to produce professional-sounding recordings.

Dynamic range compression

When people talk about "compression" in the context of tracking and mixing music they are talking specifically about dynamic range compression. At its simplest, dynamic range compression is a process whereby loud source material is made quieter and quiet source material is made louder. However, compression usually involves a lot more than simply leveling out the dynamic range of a recording. In fact, the sound imparted by compressors has been a key ingredient in every successful record of the last 45 years.

The principles of compression

Imagine you have recorded a vocal track. The vocalist has given a brilliant performance, but there's one small problem; in the four measures leading up to each chorus, the vocalist was louder than in the surrounding measures.

This is quite easy for you to fix. During mix-down, you wait for the offending loud singing and reduce the gain (volume) of the vocal track by moving the appropriate fader. You then return the fader to its original position in time for the chorus.

While making this fader-move, your brain had to make some micro-

THE THRESHOLD

This determines the level (measured in dB) of incoming signal that will trigger the compressor; the level above which the track is "too loud." Once this threshold is exceeded, the compressor will kick in and apply gain reduction. If the threshold is set too high (+10dB, for example) then a whole song might go by without the compressor kicking in and applying gain reduction. When the threshold is set low (-24dB, for example) compression will be applied nonstop.

RATIO

Ratio describes the amount of gain reduction applied by the compressor once the threshold has been reached. This value is expressed as a ratio, for example 5:1. A 5:1 ratio would mean that for every 5 dB above the threshold only 1 dB would come out of the compressor. A ratio of 1:1 would result in no gain reduction taking place; a ratio of infinity to one would mean that a threshold excess of 1000 dB coming into the compressor would be crushed to 0 dB

at the output. This extreme sort of compression is sometimes called "brick wall limiting."

GRADUAL TRANSITION

Allowing for a gradual transition from uncompressed to compressed output levels creates the impression of a more even, natural sound, especially at high ratios where a hard-knee compressor would suddenly jump on the sound and strangle it.

Compression effects

A compressor automatically takes control of the volume of a track.

Threshold

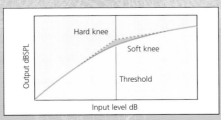

Hard knee and soft knee

>> Tech talk

Hard knee and soft knee

The term "knee" refers to the exact moment the threshold is reached and gain reduction begins. A hard knee means that the compressor will kick in suddenly when the threshold is reached. A soft knee means that signals just below and around the threshold will be compressed slightly below the set ratio, allowing for a smoother, less apparent compression. Some compressors (such as the API 2500) allow you to choose between hard and soft knee.

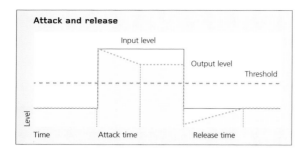

Attack and release

Input level

Output level

Threshold

Level

Time

Attack time

Release time

< **Attack:** The attack time is the time it takes for the compressor to apply gain reduction once the threshold has been reached—its "reaction time." A very fast attack time would be around 20 microseconds; a slow attack time would be around 100 milliseconds.

Release: The release time is the time it takes for the compressor to stop applying gain reduction once the signal has fallen below the threshold. A fast release time would be around 50 milliseconds; a slow release time could be as much as 5 seconds.

decisions. It had to decide at what point the singing became so loud that gain reduction was necessary. It had to decide how much gain reduction to apply and how quickly your finger should make the fader-move to apply it. Lastly, it had to decide how quickly your finger should move to return the fader to its original position once the "too loud" singing was over.

Automatic compression

A compressor is a device designed to carry out these actions automatically. Your brain and finger can't compete with a compressor when it comes to quick and precise volume reduction. And for each of the micro-decisions your brain was making when you were doing things manually, the compressor provides four user-controlled parameters. (See previous page.)

TYPES OF COMPRESSORS
VCA

Voltage-controlled amplifier (or VCA) compressors are the most commonly used kinds of compressors in modern recording. A good VCA compressor is very versatile, capable of hard limiting and gentle, transparent compression.

If you want to control dynamics accurately without coloring the sound, a VCA compressor is the answer. VCA compressors are often used to compress the mix or drum bus and the legendary SSL G Series VCA compressor is perhaps the best-known mix-bus compressor.

Opto

Compressors that use an optical isolator are often thought of as being particularly characterful compressors that can almost be used as an "effect." Opto compressors actually use an LED that responds to the level of incoming signal by glowing. The intensity of light emitted is recognised by a phototransistor and gain reduction is applied correspondingly. Because this process is inefficient in comparison with, say, VCA compression, opto compressors tend to have an idiosyncratic soft knee sound that changes

Compressor or limiter?

The term "limiter" usually describes a compressor that specializes in peak limiting, although the terms limiter and compressor are sometimes used interchangeably. Peak limiting occurs when a very high ratio of compression (at least 20:1) is applied to sudden peaks in the level of source material in order to prevent overloading (or "clipping") occurring in devices that follow the limiter in the signal path.

Limiters are particularly useful in modern recording because the sound of an overloaded analog-to-digital converter is very unpleasant; placing a limiter before your converters can help you avoid this. Limiters also have an important part to play in mastering music, ensuring that a recording is finalized at a competitive volume (see page 152).

(see page 152).

> **^ Tech talk ^**
>
> **Auto release**
> Some compressors (particularly those designed for mix-bus duties, see below) have an "auto release" function, which makes the release time dependent on several parameters (compression rate, signal levels, rate at which compression is applied) in order to avoid so-called "pumping" or "breathing." Pumping happens when compression is released too quickly, allowing a naturally decaying sound to swell and bulge unnaturally. The natural decay of different notes in a track may vary, so a fixed release time may work perfectly for the chorus while causing the verse to pump.

depending on how much gain reduction is being applied. Famous opto compressors include the Teletronix LA-2A and the Joe Meek SC2, which excel at voice and drum bus compression respectively.

FET

Compressors that use a field effect transistor (FET) for gain reduction have a distinctive, full sound and are known for their ability to apply generous amounts of gain reduction. The most famous type of FET compressor is the UREI 1176LN. Its instantly recognizable sound is on many classic recordings, from Led Zeppelin to Michael Jackson.

Vari-Mu

Vari-Mu or variable gain compressors use tubes to apply gain reduction. There aren't many Vari-Mu compressors currently in production and they are expensive, elite pieces of recording equipment. The holy grail of compressors is the vintage Fairchild 670.

Software compressors

Opinion is divided about how successful software compressors are at recreating the peculiarities of "real" compressors. What is certain is that software compressors are being used on more and more modern recordings and they are capable of doing new and exciting things. For example, software compressors can achieve attack times that are practically instantaneous and can process and analyze source material in all sorts of clever ways before applying gain reduction. TransX by Waves is one of the most innovative, a sort of multiband transient designer that can radically change source material.

Compressors buyer's guide

A selection of compressors to suit all budgets and a description of each compressor's characteristic sound.

Symetrix 501
- **Mono**
- **Budget**

The Symetrix 501 is a good-value compressor that's quiet, fully featured (there's auto release, a sidechain function, and you can link two of them together for stereo operation), and versatile. It excels at compressing bass guitar and drums and you'll be amazed at how cheaply you can pick one up if you look around.

Chameleon Labs 7720
- **Stereo**
- **Mid-priced**

The 7720 is a stereo VCA compressor designed for the mix-bus. This sort of compressor won't impose its own character on a mix, so if you want one that imparts its own color,

look elsewhere. The 7720 excels at transparent, low-ratio compression that "glues" a mix together as well as drum-bus and acoustic guitar compression.

Universal Audio 1176LN
- **Mono**
- **Expensive**

Universal Audio 1176LN is an FET compressor (strictly speaking, a limiter) that imparts a warm and distinctive "it sounds like a record!" sound to whatever is passed through it. Use it on vocals, bass, electric guitar, kick drum, room mic—just about anywhere.

Manley Vari-Mu
- **Stereo**
- **Expensive**

Mastering engineers are probably the most

demanding customers in pro-audio land. The Manley Vari-Mu is a very popular mastering suite compressor and it has been a bestseller for Manley (who make exclusively high-end gear) for a number of years. The circuit configuration is similar to the rare and costly Fairchild 670.

FMR Really Nice Compressor
- **Stereo**
- **Budget**

The RNC isn't your usual budget stereo compressor. By coupling digital controls with an all-analog signal path and a "SuperNice" mode that replicates the artifact-free, transparent compression of three compressors processing a signal in series, FMR have made a powerful, versatile, and innovative compressor that is within everyone's financial reach.

DBX 160X
- **Mono**
- **Mid-priced**

DBX no longer make the 160X (or XT) compressor, which is a

Chameleon Labs 7720

Art Pro VLA II

shame because quite a few sound engineers prefer it to DBX's current model, the 160A. If you search the secondhand market for this, you might find an outstanding bass guitar and snare drum compressor at a very attractive price.

ART Pro VLA II
- **Stereo**
- **Budget**

The VLA uses "Vactrol" optical electronics and a 12AT7 vacuum-tube gain stage to create a sound that is all its own. It's such a natural-sounding compressor that it can achieve great results on voice or piano, as well as on overheads and synths.

Chandler TG1
- **Stereo**
- **Expensive**

The custom EMI recording consoles from the late 1960s incorporated the TG12413 limiter that has been recreated by Chandler as the TG1

compressor. The TG1 sounds particularly fabulous when extreme settings are used and source material is "squashed" with a low threshold and high ratio.

Joe Meek SC2
- **Stereo**
- **Mid-priced**

Pioneering record producer Joe Meek is often credited as being the first sound engineer to realize the full potential of compression as an effect rather than a mere tool for the regulation of dynamics. "Joe Meek" the company has made compression as an effect its specialty and the SC2 (particularly its earlier revisions 1.05 and 1.07) is probably the ultimate "effect" compressor. A photo-optical design, when pushed hard it can alter the tone and rhythm of your tracks and do something different from the other compressors in your rack or DAW.

Inner Tube Audio Atomic Squeezebox
- **Stereo**
- **Fantasy island**

The Atomic Squeezebox takes unobtrusive, transparent compression to a whole new level thanks to a unique design that does not incorporate VCAs, FETs, optical, variable-Mu, or any method of gain reduction the world has ever seen before! There's no pumping, no coloration, no changing the balance of the mix or introducing unwanted artifacts—Inner Tube liken it to having a rack-mounted assistant engineer riding the faders for you!

Equalization

There's no getting around it, if you want to make a good recording you need to make use of the most powerful tool there is in audio processing: the equalizer.

Originally, the purpose of equalization was to correct or "equalize" the frequency response of a signal, and a device dedicated to this process is called an equalizer, or EQ for short. An equalizer can perform a number of important functions in the context of recording and mixing as well as live sound reinforcement, acoustic treatment, and mastering. It's a big subject, so here are the basics.

Filters

An equalizer is made up of a number of filters. These filters can increase or decrease the

amplitude of a signal within a specific frequency range; they boost and cut specific frequencies. Exactly how wide that frequency range is and how much increase or decrease in amplitude can be applied depends on the type of filter used and the design of the equalizer in question.

Imagine you are presented with an acoustic guitar track that is a real "keeper." The only problem is that a large truck drove by while the guitarist was recording it, creating an annoying rumbling noise in the middle of the track. Rather than getting the guitarist to

PEAKING FILTER

Imagine that you have intrusive noise coming from the hum of a refrigerator. You could try eliminating the noise with a high-pass filter, but this probably wouldn't be effective. In order to eliminate the refrigerator noise you are going to need an EQ that employs a peaking filter. There are three user-controlled parameters associated with a peaking filter:

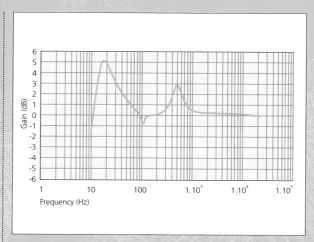

Peaking filter frequency response

High-pass filter

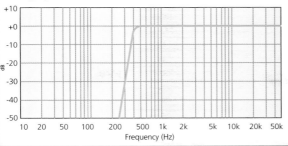

High-pass filter

A high-pass filter only allows frequencies above a user-defined cut-off point to pass. Frequencies directly below the cut-off point will be drastically "rolled-off," and frequencies farther below the cut-off point that are beyond the "roll-off" phase of filtering will be eliminated completely.

High-pass filter
A high-pass filter only allows frequencies above a user-defined cut-off point to pass. Frequencies directly below the cut-off point will be drastically "rolled-off," and frequencies farther below the cut-off point that are beyond the "roll-off" phase of filtering will be eliminated completely.

Frequency, *which determines the center frequency that will be boosted or cut.*

Gain, *which determines how much positive (boost) or negative (cut) gain will be applied to the selected frequency.*

Q *(sometimes called resonance or bandwidth), which determines the width of the band of frequencies affected by the filter.*

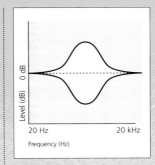

Average Q
A peaking filter allows you to cut or boost a limited band of adjacent frequencies. Here a 10 dB boost is applied with an average Q value at 750 Hz, whereas...

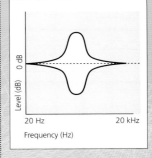

High Q
...here the Q is much higher. Note that fewer frequencies adjacent to the designated center frequency are affected by the boost.

re-record his part, you could use an EQ to eliminate the rumble. It's a safe bet that the offending rumble is concentrated in the lower frequencies, so you would try to use an EQ that has a high-pass filter. A cut-off point of 100Hz would probably eliminate most of the rumble without interfering with the sound of the acoustic guitar.

Another type of filter is the peaking filter, and its functions are explained in more detail in the box at the bottom of page 64.

The shelving filter is one other type of filter which is commonly used in equalization. Shelving filters come in two forms: the high-shelf filter and the low-shelf filter. A high-shelf filter will cut or boost all frequencies above a user-defined point. A low-shelf filter will cut or boost all frequencies below a user-defined point.

GRAPHIC EQUALIZERS

A graphic equalizer consists of a large number of peaking filters (often as many as 30) that have a pre-determined center frequency and Q. Graphic EQs are typically used in the context of live music, but there are some graphic EQs that are commonly used in recording, such as the API 560EQ.

Parametric equalizers

A fully parametric equalizer consists of a small number of peaking filters (usually four or five) that have an adjustable center frequency and Q. Because these parameters are user-defined, the parametric EQ offers greater power and control than a graphic EQ, and the vast majority of EQs found in recording studios are parametric.

Many parametric EQs feature high and low-shelf filters as well as peaking filters. EQs of this kind that have a fixed Q are called semi-parametric equalizers.

Software equalizers

Software EQs are generally designed to work in the same way as parametric EQs, offering the user a combination of peaking and shelving filters.

CANCEL UNWANTED NOISE USING EQ

> *Record your part.*
> *You may find afterward that there is unwanted noise in the background, such as a truck passing by, or muttering.*
> *Identify the offending frequency of the sound by setting a peaking filter to a high boost, then moving the frequency around until the sound you don't want is at its most audible.*
> *Cut the gain on that EQ band and adjust the Q until it sounds good to you.*
> *If the sound is very low-or high-pitched, try high- or low-pass filters; they might produce a better result.*

∧ > EQ in Logic
EQ is typically visualized as an interactive graph with peaks and troughs depicting your various cuts and boosts and the Q involved.

Equalizers buyer's guide

A selection of EQs
to suit all budgets
and applications.

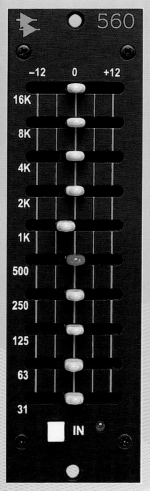

API 560 EQ

API 560 EQ
- **Mid-priced**
- **Mono graphic EQ**

The API 560 EQ never
ceases to surprise sound
engineers who have
become accustomed to
the idea that parametric
equals better. The 560
applies a "proportional Q"
that widens the frequency
bandwidth at lower boost/
cut levels and narrows
the bandwidth (applies a
higher Q setting) at higher
boost/cut levels.

Focusrite Green 2
- **Mid-priced (secondhand)**
- **Focus EQ**
- **Mono parametric EQ**

Focusrite are famous
for their Rupert Neve-
designed ISA preamps
and the Red Series EQ.
The Green EQ is clean
and musical, so much
so that the sound retains
its integrity and sounds
natural at high cut/
boost settings, which is
the hallmark of a good
equalizer.

Klark Teknik DN410
- **Mid-priced (secondhand)**
- **Stereo parametric EQ**

This EQ is commonly used
in a live sound context and
more rarely for recording,
but don't let that put you
off. This is a clean, flexible
equalizer that can operate
in dual-mono mode as well
as in stereo, and can also
become a single 10-band
mono equalizer if required.
Each filter can operate
across a frequency
spectrum that ranges from
20Hz to 20kHz, ideal for
corrective equalization.

Tech talk

The 500 series format
*Outboard gear doesn't always come in a standard
19-in (48-cm) rack-mounted format. 500-series units
come in a 5¼ x 1½ in (13.5 x 4 cm) format that
can be mounted vertically in a specially designed
"lunchbox" designed to house and power a small
number of them. A host of manufacturers support
the 500 series, including Chandler, Buzz Audio, Purple
Audio, and Empirical Labs.*

Klark Teknik DN410

GML 8200

- **Expensive**
- **Stereo parametric EQ**

This unit is the closest thing there is to an industry-standard mix-bus equalizer. Legendary producer George Massenburg is credited with inventing the concept of parametric equalization (GML is his company) and the 8200 is hard to beat. This unit excels at surgical, precise equalization and when high frequencies are boosted, a beautiful "air" can be added to the signal without any associated harshness or brittleness.

A-Design Hammer EQ

- **Expensive**
- **Stereo parametric EQ**

The Hammer EQ is a relative newcomer, but it has gained a big reputation in record time thanks to its larger-than-life sound. The Hammer is a dual-mono three-band tube equalizer that follows in the tradition of the best vacuum tube audio gear by making everything passed through it sound that little bit bigger, even

when all the filters are set to zero! It doesn't excel as a surgical EQ, but if you want lashings of musicality and punch, the Hammer is a great choice.

Chandler Germanium Tone Control

- **Expensive**
- **Mono EQ**

The Germanium Tone Control is a throwback to the 1960s when products by Neve, Fairchild, EMI, and Telefunken (among others) all used germanium transistors. But this unit is far from being merely a retro curiosity. The Tone Control has a unique design that categorizes its three filters

into "Thick," "Presence," and "Treble" categories, and there are feedback and drive controls that can add a musical, solid-state distortion to your music.

Esoteric Audio Research (EAR) 822 Pultec Style EQ

- **Fantasy island**
- **Mono program EQ**

Tim de Paravicini's biography on EAR's website states that in order for Tim to manufacture a product, he must be convinced that its design is superior to anything else out there that does the same job. Tim is a highly esteemed technician and designer and the 822 is perhaps the only Pultec-style EQ that can claim to be as good or even better than an original Pultec.

Tech talk

EQ on a budget
So... why no budget EQs? There are cheap outboard EQs out there, of course, but the truth is that such units usually don't offer any significant benefit over the built in equalizers contained in your DAW or mixing desk. If you wanted to expand your EQ options on a tight budget, your best bet would be to invest in plug-in EQs that can process your music ITB ("in the box," see page 81). Waves' Renaissance EQ, Massey Plugins' vt3 EQ, and Sonnox's Oxford EQ are good examples of software EQs that have been used on countless hit records and are in some instances preferable to traditional hardware equalization.

Interfaces and converters

A detailed account of analog to digital
conversion would be about as long and complicated
as a seminar on advanced physics. But if you
intend to record your music to a computer or
hard disk recorder, you need to understand
some of the basics.

There are loads of products out
there that allow you to record music
directly onto your computer or
hard drive. There are mixing desks
that interface with your computer via
FireWire, preamps with digital outputs
that can connect to a soundcard
inside your computer; there are even
microphones that plug directly into a
USB port. What all of these products
have in common is something called
"conversion," a process that changes
an analog signal into a sequence of
numbers. Specifically, this process is
called analog to digital conversion, or
A/D conversion. The process of turning
numbers (digital) back into an analog
signal is called digital to analog
conversion, or D/A conversion.

What's the difference?

So what's the difference between
analog and digital equipment? Well,
any piece of equipment—from a
microphone to a compressor to a
speaker—that processes a continuously
variable signal (sound or electricity)
into another continuously variable
signal is known as an analog piece of
equipment: The output is an "analog" of
the input. "Continuously variable" is the
main selling point of analog.

A digital circuit, on the other hand,
processes code; it thinks in terms of
numbers and nothing else. Any piece
of equipment that processes numbers
into other numbers is called digital
because it deals exclusively with
digits (zeros and ones).

HOW IT WORKS

On the right (top) you can
see a visual representation
of an analog signal, that is,
a signal whose voltage
(Y axis) varies over time
(X axis).

Now you need to turn
this into numbers for your
digital gear. In order to get
numbers out of an analog
signal, an A/D converter's
circuit takes snapshot
"samples" of the voltage

as time progresses.
Each sample is recorded
as a number, and
each number varies
depending on the level of
voltage. Below right is a
visualization of another
signal, this time showing
the various points along
the time axis at which a
sample is taken.

The problem is,
the analog signal is
continuously variable,

changing all the time in
complex, unpredictable
ways. Any quantification
of this signal is going to
be a mere approximation
because time is an
infinitely reducible value—
no matter how many
numbers you use, you will
never arrive at a perfect
quantification of time.
For example, you could
take snapshots that are
closer together. But it's still

There is nothing particularly esoteric about devices that convert analog to digital and vice versa. If you own a CD player then you own a D/A converter; every CD player has one so that the digital information on a CD can be turned into a voltage that can then be amplified and fed into a pair of speakers or headphones. Modern telephones use converters, too.

However, not all converters were created equal... Your choice of A/D and D/A converter will affect the quality of your recordings. So if you care about your music, then you need to care about the details of how your sounds will be turned into numbers and then back into sound.

Resolution and sampling rate

Resolution determines the accuracy at which the voltage is sampled. It is measured in bits and is sometimes referred to as a "bit-depth resolution." Using a low resolution is a bit like giving prices in dollars and leaving out the cents. The higher your bit-count, the higher the resolution. Audio is encoded on a CD at a 16-bit resolution.

A "bit" is nothing more than a binary digit, that is, a one or a zero. If a sample is taken at an 8-bit resolution it means that there are 256 values that can be used to describe the sample voltage (8-bit = 2 to the power of 8 = 256). A 16-bit resolution would mean that

an approximation, just a slightly better one. What's increased in this case is the sampling rate, which is measured in kHz. A higher sampling rate means greater accuracy in approximating the wave form in digits. See the diagrams on page 72. This, along with digital resolution, is one of the two key concepts in digital conversion.

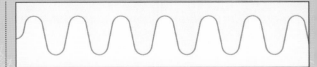

An analog signal is curvy and smooth.

A digital signal varies in little steps rather than continuously—this way it can be expressed in numbers.

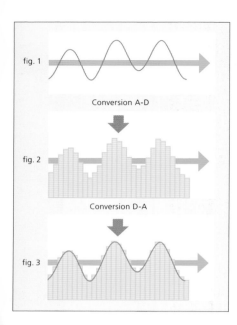

‹ Conversion
These diagrams illustrate the nature of an analog signal (fig. 1), a digital representation of that signal (fig. 2), and conversion back to analog (fig. 3).

fig. 1

Conversion A-D

fig. 2

Conversion D-A

fig. 3

65,536 values could be applied to signify that same voltage (16-bit = 2 to the power of 16 = 65,536). If you ever get the chance to compare the results of an 8-bit with a 16-bit A/D conversion you will hear a dramatic difference in quality. "Sampling rate" refers to the number of samples that are taken in any given period of time. This is usually measured in kHz, that is, thousand instances per second. The sampling rate of CD audio is 44.1 kHz, which means that the original (analog) audio was sampled 44,100 times per second when A/D conversion took place.

SNR AND BIT-DEPTH RESOLUTION

The average signal-to-noise ratio (SNR) of a piece of analog audio equipment effectively describes its dynamic range. The quieter you can get your signal without noise drowning it out, the more dynamic range you have at your disposal. Converters also have SNR; the noise is the error signal caused by quantizing. The lower the bit rate, the greater the inaccuracies, and the more pronounced the error. This will increase the SNR and reduce dynamic range. Higher bit-depth resolution means greater dynamic range once the audio is converted back to analog. The rule is that for every "bit" of resolution, you gain c.6dB of dynamic range. So a 12-bit resolution results in a SNR of c.72dB; a 16-bit resolution gives an SNR of c.96db.

The issue is that very few (analog) sound reproduction systems are able to produce a dynamic range of more than 120 dB, so there is no practical benefit in increasing the resolution of a converter beyond 20 bits. Most commercial studios record at a 24-bit resolution, allowing for a dynamic range of c.144 dB. In these situations the analog stage of the converters themselves will usually limit the dynamic range of audio to c.120 dB.

Sampling rate

The most important idea in the history of sampling is the Nyquist-Shannon sampling theorem. In order to capture a particular audio frequency you must sample at a rate that is double that of the frequency in question. So the CD-quality sampling rate of 44.1 kHz is theoretically able to capture frequencies up to and including 22.05 kHz, which is perfect for

Digital output
An electric guitar produces a digital signal.

domestic use because most hi-fis and headphones are unable to reproduce frequencies above c.20 kHz.

So why would you want a converter with a sampling rate that reproduces frequencies higher than 22.05kHz? For a number of reasons, a conversion process will ideally use a sampling rate that encompasses the very upper frequency range of what high-end microphones can detect and very high-spec monitors can reproduce—around 40kHz. A sampling rate of 88.2kHz will achieve this; the 96kHz rate used professionally is overkill.

So what of the lightning-fast sampling rates that are possible with the present generation of converters, as high as 192 kHz? Some say the sound of 192 kHz is audibly superior to 96 kHz; others argue that 192kHz has no benefits and causes problems in the conversion process that are detrimental to sound quality.

‹ CD sampling rate
CD-quality sampling rate is compatible with most domestic hi-fis and headphones.

More is better... or is it?

In theory, the higher the resolution and the higher the sampling rate, the more faithful the digitization will be to the original analog signal. You would literally be capturing more of the analog signal, with a higher number of samples per second and a more complex numeric representation of each sample. So, the ideal A/D converter for you would have a sampling rate that's stupidly fast and a bit-depth resolution that's astronomically high… right?

Well, the truth is a little bit more complicated. There are two real-world considerations that are sometimes overlooked: The signal-to-noise ratio (SNR) of analog equipment and the range of frequencies that the human ear can hear (see previous page).

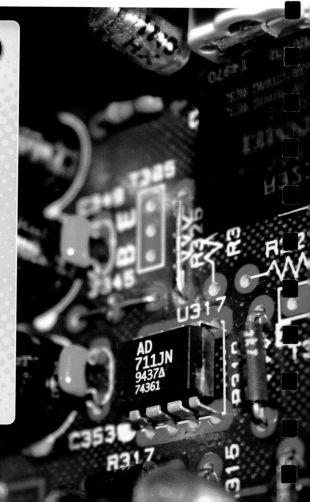

SUMMARY

There are details of the A/D and D/A conversion process that are beyond the scope of this book, but that are crucial to the quality of a converter. Issues such as anti-aliasing filters, quantization error, and dither will all affect your music, not to mention the specification of a converter's analog qualities. Converters are analog devices as well as digital and impart their own quality to a signal in the same way as any piece of analog gear.

Also bear in mind that the greater the resolution and sampling rate, the more hard disk space and processing power you will need. This is a serious consideration when choosing the right converter for your home studio because a sampling rate of 96kHz is likely to halve your track count in Logic or Pro Tools when compared to the default 48kHz, for example.

Interfaces and converters buyer's guide

A selection of interfaces and converters to suit different budgets and recording needs.

Apogee Duet FireWire interface
- **Budget**
- **2-channel**

Apogee are heavyweights in the field of A/D–D/A converters, and their high-end multichannel converters can be found in recording studios the world over. The Duet is extraordinary in the sense that it allows you to obtain true Apogee sound quality on a low budget. The Duet might not have the range of features of some of its rivals, but what it does do, it does very well indeed. The fact that it is slimline, portable, and functions as an outstanding microphone preamplifier is a bonus. The downside is that it's designed to work with Apple computers running Logic, Soundtrack Pro, or GarageBand only.

Lynx Aurora 16 A/D–D/A converter
- **Expensive**
- **16-channel**

This unit may be classed as "expensive," but it's possible that the Aurora 16 offers greater value for money than any other converter out there. That's because it doesn't just offer 16 channels of simultaneous A/D and D/A conversion, it offers 16 channels of very high-quality conversion; conversion of such quality that an increasing number of the world's top studios are using the Aurora in place of converters by Digidesign and Apogee, for example. If you are looking to record and process several channels at once, the Aurora is a great choice.

E-MU 0404 USB interface
- **Budget**
- **2-channel**

If your budget is tight, or you want to add a portable interface to your existing setup, the 0404 is a straightforward two-channel A/D–D/A converter equipped with fully featured preamps. It's a USB interface, so setup is as simple as could be, and with an onboard MIDI interface and Hi-Z inputs for direct electric guitar/bass recording you have an impressive unit that punches above its price bracket.

Audient Mico mic pre and converter
- **Mid-priced**
- **2-channel**

The Mico is firmly aimed at desktop users looking for a compact, integrated "front end" for their setup. Audient are best known as a manufacturer of mixing desks, so they know a thing or two about how to make a good preamp. The preamps on the Mico are the same discrete class-A designs found in Audient's ASP8024 console and they include such unusual features as "HMX" harmonic sculpting technology and variphase control. These allow the user to dial in musical harmonics (such as those that might be introduced by classic tube gear) and adjust the phase alignment of the two signals respectively.

All-in-one solutions buyer's guide

Hardware interfaces and converters often come as part of a multipurpose unit—complete with faders, preamps, or even EQ. These units are loosely known as controllers, mixers, or mixing desks.

Mackie Onyx 1640 + FireWire card
- **Mid-priced**
- **16 channel**

Mackie have a reputation for building reliable, hardy, and relatively inexpensive mixers among other recording and live sound equipment. The Onyx is a feature-rich mixing console with surprisingly good preamps, six aux sends, and four-band EQ on each channel, a dedicated talkback section, and bombproof build quality overall. The conversion from the optional FireWire card might not bear comparison with something in the league of the Lynx converters listed here, but this is a such a great little unit that it could be used as an analog mixer going into outboard converters if you decided to upgrade your setup.

Tascam FW1082 firewire control surface and audio interface
- **Mid-priced**
- **10-channel**

The 1082 has been around for a few years now, so you might be able to find one secondhand. It provides 10-in/4-out conversion at 96kHz and a fully featured control surface designed to work with Logic, Cubase (Cubase LE comes packaged with the unit), Nuendo, and Ableton Live. Tascam products are known for their reliability, and some of the features on offer here are surprising at the price, such as touch-sensitive motorized faders and the ability to control video editing software Final Cut Pro.

Allen and Heath Zed R16 audio interface, control surface and analog mixer
- **Expensive**
- **18-channel**

In the future you'll be seeing more and more units like this one, an all-in-one solution to the home studio-owner's recording needs. Allen

Mackie Onyx 1640 + FireWire card

Tascam FW1082

Weiss Engineering ADC-2 converter

and Heath are known for their transparent, reliable mixing desks designed for use in live sound application, and the R16 is their first mixing desk designed specifically for recording in more than ten years. As well as 18 channels of conversion both ways (that is, A/D and D/A) via FireWire, the R16 is a proper analog mixing console, complete with insert points, preamps, and EQs on each channel, and built-in talkback. Not only that, it functions as a MIDI controller, too, so you can make adjustments to plug-ins inside your DAW directly.

Weiss Engineering ADC-2 converter
- **Fantasy island**
- **2-channel**

As you might imagine, the stereo A/D converters commonly used in mastering suites are among the very best available. Converters by Lavry, Prism, and Crane Song spring to mind as being regarded as the best of the best, but perhaps the most uncompromising, elite converters of all are those designed by Daniel Weiss in Switzerland. The ADC-2 offers the user unsurpassed transparency and fidelity to the source, and it is regarded by many as the finest converter money can buy.

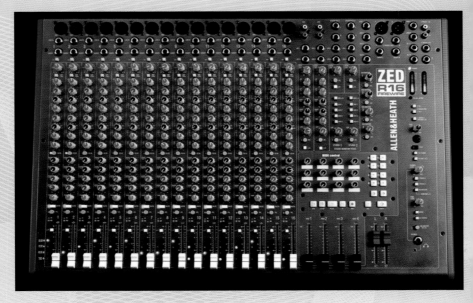

Allen and Heath Zed R16 audio interface, control surface, and analog mixer

Digital audio workstations

Choosing the right digital audio workstation (DAW) for your needs can be tough. The main contenders such as Logic, Nuendo, and Pro Tools have all been used to produce loads of hits and any one of them can produce stellar results in any genre.

Multitrack recording

In the 1940s, guitarist and engineer Les Paul developed a new recording technique known as "multitrack recording," and by the 1960s it had become the norm. This technology enables you to record sound sources separately and "mix" them into a balanced whole.

You can record different tracks of your song (guitar, voice, bass, drums) one at a time, and gradually layer them on top of each other. This is known as "overdubbing."

Even if you choose to record your song with several layers playing at once (acoustic guitar and voice, for example), you can still record them onto separate tracks using separate microphones. This allows you to adjust the volume level of each track afterward and to process and add effects to individual tracks.

Before multitrack recording, all instruments and voices had to be recorded at the same time, and any balancing in volume (singer being too loud, bass too light, and so on) had to be engineered at the recording stage and couldn't be

HOW TO DECIDE

It's possible that mundane practical considerations will make a choice of DAW for you. For example, your collaborator might use Apple's Logic, so Logic would be the obvious choice; or it could be that you intend to do a lot of work at a local recording studio that uses Steinberg's Nuendo, so you decide to use Nuendo or another piece of Steinberg software, Cubase. There are, however, some differences between the DAWs that

you should know about. For the purposes of this book, Apple's Logic, Steinberg's Nuendo and Digidesign's Pro Tools will be examined,

DAW tracking
DAWs present a multitrack project as a series of stacked horizontal bars.

altered once recorded ("Oh no!
You can't hear the trumpet on this
recording… we'll have to do the
whole thing again.").

Typical setup
*A typical computer-based recording setup
with two different keyboards and acoustic
guitars for greater versatility.*

but there is also other
DAW software out there
such as Sonar, Reason, and
Ableton Live.

Logic
The history and evolution
of Logic stretches back
to the 1980s when a piece
of software called Notator
was made by C-Labs,
who would later become
E-Magic before being
taken over by Apple in
2002. The important
thing to remember about
Logic is that it started life
as a sequencer, a way of
ordering and controlling

MIDI events rather than
recording and editing
audio. While the current
incarnation of Logic ("Logic
Studio") can record and
edit audio brilliantly, it is
its supreme MIDI-
friendliness that makes
it a favorite of those
producing electronic or
sample-based music
of all genres.
   Logic Studio is probably
the best value-for-money
product in the history of
recording. For a relatively
inexpensive piece of
software, the range
and quality of facilities

offered by Logic Studio is
staggering and without
rival. For example, Logic
Studio includes compressor,
reverb, and delay plug-ins
that are as good as any
available. It also includes
a huge library of samples
and loops, as well as a
selection of soft-synths and
virtual instruments that
make extremely powerful
production tools.
   For the price, Logic
Studio has no drawbacks
as such. But for all of its
virtues, it is not the ideal
DAW for everyone. Logic
can only run on Apple

DAW basics

A DAW is, at its simplest, a digital replacement for the multitrack tape machine. You can record and play back multiple tracks simultaneously and make "cut and paste" edits to audio just as you would with multitrack tape. Of course, storing and editing data in the digital domain has all sorts of advantages. Engineers accustomed to working with tape sometimes prefer this sort of straightforward DAW, the most popular example of which is iZ's Radar V, which offers integrated A/D–D/A conversion and ultra-reliable performance without the need for a Mac or PC-style computer.

As computers have become more powerful, DAW software capable of turning a normal domestic computer

computers, and it requires a powerful Mac to make the most of its features. Critically, Logic is still lagging behind Pro Tools in terms of its ability to record live instruments and edit recorded tracks with speed and efficiency. For these reasons, Pro Tools remains the industry standard DAW.

PRO TOOLS

Pro Tools is the only computer-based DAW that was designed to be, first and foremost, a tool for multitrack recording and editing. The flagship Pro Tools HD is the most commonly found DAW in commercial recording facilities, and from a traditional sound engineering perspective it offers an intuitive "flow"—both workflow and signal-flow. The editing power of Pro Tools HD is unparalleled, allowing users to radically manipulate the pitch and rhythm of recorded tracks.

For example, a drum part consisting of 12 different individual tracks (a track for snare, one for kick, one for hi-hat, and so on) can have its timing "corrected" at the touch of a button. The downside of Pro Tools HD is its price, or rather the price of the DSP cards that are required to run HD, which home users might find difficult to justify. Digidesign introduced Pro Tools LE and Pro Tools M-Powered for this reason, and of course recordings made on any Pro Tools software have the advantage of easy transferability to your local recording studio, which is probably running Pro Tools HD. The drawback of LE and M-Powered is the limited range of A/D converters that are able to interface with the software. In summary, Pro Tools should be seriously considered by anyone (a four-piece rock band, for example) focused on

tracking live instruments and editing the recorded tracks, and Pro Tools HD is a good investment if you are planning to offer your services recording other people's music or branch out into sound engineering.

Nuendo

Steinberg are famous for Cubase, a piece of software that, like Logic, started out as a MIDI sequencer before becoming the fully-fledged DAW and recording tool it is today. Today, Steinberg's flagship DAW is Nuendo, which offers superb audio post-production facilities that are ideal for editing music and dialog for film. Nuendo is a common tool in the motion picture and television industries, as you might expect, but it also has a growing fanbase among recording studio engineers and music producers for its intelligent user interface, flexibility, and clever routing options. Like Logic, Nuendo requires a powerful

into a tool for recording and editing music has become more and more ambitious, offering facilities that are less like a multitrack tape machine and more like a fully-equipped recording studio. For example, Pro Tools doesn't just allow you to make simple edits and record multiple tracks. It allows you to process audio with EQ, compression, and effects within the computer. Once you have recorded your raw tracks to Pro Tools, the entire production can be carried out inside the computer, from complex editing to mixing to mastering. This is known as working "in the box," or ITB.

Pro Tools
Pro Tools is the most commonly found DAW in the music industry.

computer to make the most of its features, although it can run on both PCs and Macs. The price of Nuendo might put some users off and Steinberg's Cubase makes an excellent, cheaper, alternative.

Integrated DAWs
An integrated DAW offers a complete recording solution in one package. A good example is the Roland VS-2000CD, which provides a mixing console, preamps, A/D-D/A conversion, hard disk recording, and software for editing in one neat package. These individual components might not be the best examples of their type, but that's not the point. If you're looking for a hassle-free, cost-effective way of recording your music without the inevitable problems associated with PCs and Macs, then an integrated DAW might just be for you.

Monitors

Monitors are speakers designed especially for tracking and mixing music. Monitors differ from domestic hi-fi speakers in one important way: While speakers are designed to flatter source material and make it sound good, monitors are designed to be revealing and unforgiving.

This fundamental difference aside, it is very difficult to generalize about what distinguishes monitors from the speakers in your lounge. It is often said that monitors are relatively neutral, exhibiting a flatter frequency response than hi-fi speakers and, while this is not always the case, monitors do tend to produce a less "hyped" sound than hi-fi speakers. Monitors also tend to have a wider frequency bandwidth as well as being heavier and more robust than comparably priced hi-fi speakers.

Ultimately, the music you record will be listened to on headphones and hi-fi speakers, so why shouldn't you record and mix using these? The reality is that the speakers in your house are different from the speakers in your neighbor's house, which are in turn different from the speakers in your local bar. A mix that sounds good on your speakers (which might have a "hyped" heightened frequency response between 150–350 hz, for example) could end up sounding thin and unimpressive on your neighbor's system. The only surefire way to produce music that will sound good on different systems and in different environments is to record and mix in an acoustically controlled environment through a pair of monitors.

Small, medium, or large

The impressive-looking monitors you'll find in large commercial recording facilities are known as "mains," short for main control room monitors. A good pair of mains will typically have superb off-axis frequency response, a very wide frequency bandwidth, and superlative imaging and dynamics. A mains monitor will often use four or five drivers (a typical domestic speaker uses two, sometimes referred to as woofer and tweeter) connected up to a power amplifier that is almost

▶I) TOP TIP

Midfield monitors are the bigger, bassier brothers of nearfields. Consider a pair of midfields, especially if you're working in a medium- to large-sized room.

as big as the monitors themselves! Mains are designed and built with no expense spared to reproduce audio in the most revealing and critical way possible, which should make them the listening source most likely to yield a good mix.

Funnily enough, though, there is a consensus among mix engineers that mixing exclusively on mains often results in a final product that doesn't translate well to domestic systems. It would seem that the uncompromising design of main monitors and the not-so-uncompromising design of domestic sound reproduction systems are just too disparate. This is where nearfield monitors come in…

Nearfield monitors

Nearfield monitors are small speakers intended to be listened to in the "near-field," positioned in close proximity to the listener. For the last 25 years, nearfield monitors have been indispensable tools of the mix engineer. In fact, an increasing number of records are mixed almost exclusively on nearfield monitors.

One advantage of nearfield monitors is that their close proximity to the listener—usually within 6 ft (2 m)—means that sound emanating directly from them is much more prominent than indirect, reflected sound. A good pair of nearfields can be analytical and unforgiving at the same time as helping engineers to produce mixes that translate to car stereos, earbuds, computer speakers, and domestic systems in general.

TO WOOF OR NOT TO WOOF

If you are planning to record bass-heavy material such as hip-hop or dance music, you should seriously consider adding an active subwoofer to your monitors. A subwoofer is a speaker dedicated to reproducing frequencies between c.20 Hz and c.150 Hz exclusively.

Monitors buyer's guide

Auditioning hi-fi speakers is easy. You're listening for an enjoyable, full, musical sound. But how do you go about auditioning a pair of monitors when a consistently full, "nice" sound can compromise the recording and mixing process?

Things to listen out for

The word to keep in mind here is "detail." The more clearly defined each instrument is in the mix the better, as this will make it easier for you to make decisions about EQ and levels. Low frequencies should sound tight and "fast," and expect high frequencies to sound more prominent than they would on conventional hi-fi speakers. You should also listen out for a sense of depth in the music with some elements sounding more "forward" than others. This will give you a good indication of how well the monitors elucidate the dynamic range of a mix and ultimately how well you will be able to make critical mixing decisions regarding levels and compression.

LISTENING MATERIAL

Whether you're auditioning monitors in your home studio (this is ideal) or elsewhere, it is important to use well-chosen demo material. Music you have recorded yourself and music you are very familiar with would be good choices, but there are also some classic albums that are generally accepted as being exceptionally well-produced and having a wonderful "sound." Try albums such as:

- *• **Dark Side Of The Moon** (1973) by Pink Floyd (produced by Pink Floyd, engineered by Alan Parsons)*

- *• **Hotel California** (1976) by The Eagles (produced by Bill Symczyk)*

- *• **Thriller** by Michael Jackson (produced by Quincy Jones, engineered by Bruce Swedien)*

- *• **ok computer** by Radiohead (produced by Nigel Godrich)*

Monitors
A pair of studio monitors. For advice on what to listen for, see the panel, right.

AUDITIONING MONITORS

Ask yourself these questions:

- *How clearly can I distinguish reverbs and delays from other elements in the mix?*
- *How effective is the stereo imaging— do instruments have their own "place" in the stereo field?*
- *When I increase the volume, does the sound retain its integrity and balance without any distortion or loss of quality? (You should only do this within reasonable limits and for very short periods.)*
- *Can I hear questionable production decisions clearly? A good pair of monitors will allow you to assess the dubious merits of the headphone bleed on Christina Aguilera's Beautiful and the excessive compression of Metallica's album Death Magnetic, for example.*
- *Do different recordings sound really different? A good pair of monitors might give you a new appreciation of the sonic "fingerprint" each album carries.*

- **Continuum** *by John Mayer (produced by John Mayer and Steve Jordan, mixed by Manny Marroquin and Michael Brauer)*

Elaborate pop productions such as Britney Spears' **Toxic** *and Usher's* **Love In This Club** *make good "wild-cards" to bring to an audition.*

Adam A7

Adam A7
• Mid-priced

The Adam A7 is a serious monitor that can be found in high-end recording studios as well as home recording setups. This Berlin-based company has been making acclaimed studio monitors since 1999, implementing their innovative Accelerating Ribbon Technology (ART) to create high-frequency drivers that are smooth and non-fatiguing.

Klein and Hummel 0300
• Expensive

If you can stretch your budget, there is no single product that will improve your every recording and mixing decision like a top-class pair of nearfields. The 0300 uses a three-way system, comprising treble, mid-range, and bass drivers. Tremendous care has been taken to ensure that this monitor is neutral, powerful, and as free as possible from unwanted resonance. All in all, the design is uncompromising and so is the sound. If you audition the 0300s, bring along a wide range of material and all will be revealed…

Yamaha NS-10M
• Budget

Where to start… The story of Yamaha's NS-10 nearfield monitor is perhaps the most interesting of any piece of professional audio equipment. Manufactured between 1978 and 2001, the NS-10 became the only monitor in history that could be found in the majority of recording studios. Look at a photo of a studio control room and the chances are that you will be able to make out a pair of small, black speakers with white woofers sitting over the console's meter bridge. How did a small, relatively inexpensive monitor become so indispensable?

NS-10s are by no means neutral-sounding, they have poor bass extension, and a fatiguing, aggressive top end. Worst of all, they don't do a good job at conveying a sense of dynamic range and are likely to obscure the line between compression and over-compression compared to other, more expensive monitors. But in the 1980s, engineers realized that mixing on NS-10s resulted in mixes that translated exceptionally well to domestic systems. In fact, the consensus emerged that if it sounded good on NS-10s, it would sound good anywhere.

There is no straightforward way of explaining why NS-10s are so good at helping to create commercially successful records. Perhaps it's because they act as a magnifying glass on the mid-range, emphasizing frequencies that car stereos and hi-fis tend to de-emphasize. Whatever the reason, the NS-10s legendary status is undeniable. If you are looking to own just one pair of monitors then you should look elsewhere, but if you are looking for a pair of nearfields to complement a larger pair of monitors like the PMC TB2S-As then NS-10s are ideal. Bear in mind that you will have to budget for an amplifier to power them (the Yamaha P2500 is good) and that you may need to replace both the bass and treble drivers if you are buying a pair that has seen a lot of use.

Mackie HR824 mkII
• **Mid-priced**
Mackie are famous for their rugged, no-nonsense mixers, but that doesn't mean they can't make a cracking monitor. The 824 is a larger example of the nearfield variety, weighing in at 34.6 lb (15.7 kg) with an 8¾-in (22-cm) woofer that helps to achieve a smooth frequency response from 20 kHz all the way down to an impressive 35 Hz. If you are recording pop, RnB, or hip-hop, 824s should definitely be on your audition list.

PMC TB2S-A
• **Expensive**
Phone up your local sound engineer and ask him to name the three companies he thinks of as providing the very, very best in studio monitoring. You can bet that one of those names will be PMC and there are few (if any) active midfield monitors that can outdo the TB2S-A in its price range. This is partly due to the ingenious "Flying Mole" digital amplifier that powers it with 160 watts into 4 ohms

despite weighing just 1.4 lb (650 g)!

Yamaha MSP5
• **Budget**
There is disagreement about whether cheap studio monitors are worth buying. But if you are on a tight budget and you can't stretch to the mid-priced monitors made by Adam, Dynaudio, or Genelec, then you could do a lot worse than a pair of Yamaha MSP5s. At this price, you can't really go wrong.

KRK VXT4
• **Budget**
Another small budget monitor… If you're working in a small space, this self-amplified monitor is forward, and has a good tonal balance and a sturdy build. KRK have a good reputation and their now-defunct V6 has been used by super-producer Timbaland, among others.

Dynaudio BM5
• **Mid-priced**
Dynaudio have a reputation for producing transparent, analytical monitors and the BM5 definitely falls into that category. One of Dynaudio's bestselling monitors, the BM5 is available either as an active or a passive

monitor, and those with medium-sized spaces and slightly bigger budgets should be sure to check out the larger BM6.

ATC SCM110A SL PRO
• **Fantasy island**
Here on fantasy island there is only one choice of monitor manufacturer, the Acoustic Transducer Company, or ATC. The company is based in Gloucestershire, UK, and it has been run by its founder William Woodman since 1974. Take a look at the equipment lists of Europe's top studios and you will find ATCs in abundance. They are not quite as prevalent in US studios (yet…) but their reputation is second to none.

Chapter 3

Combining equipment

The way you link up and position your equipment will have a big impact on the way you work. You need to keep in mind what it is you want to achieve with your recordings and build up a collection of complementary equipment that can match your expectations.

Some typical setups

When putting your studio together you should remember this axiom: your signal path is only as good as the weakest link in the chain. In other words, you should think twice about forking out money on a very expensive Gefell microphone and Manley compressor if you intend to use them with bargain-basement preamps and converters. With this in mind, on the following pages are three setups that are well balanced in terms of the quality of their constituent elements.

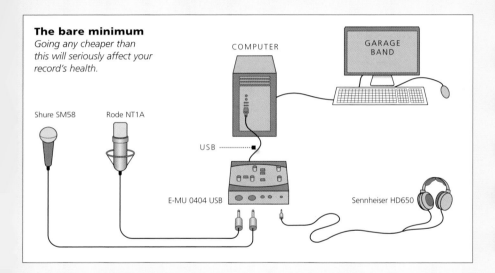

The bare minimum
Going any cheaper than this will seriously affect your record's health.

COMPUTER

GARAGE BAND

Shure SM58   Rode NT1A

USB ·············

E-MU 0404 USB

Sennheiser HD650

On the cheap

1 This is a solid, thrifty setup, perfect for getting a demo down quickly. The SM58 and NT1A offer you the choice of dynamic and condenser mic respectively and both are good mics for recording vocals. The DAW is Apple's GarageBand, which comes free with every new Apple Mac as part of the iLife package. If you are a PC user, Cubase Essential 4 or even the free recording and sound-editing program Audacity could serve as substitutes. As for monitoring, headphones are not ideal and they can't be relied upon to give you a sense of how your mix will translate to other systems. However, on a very tight budget there are no speakers that will compete with the HD650s in terms of detail and fidelity. The E-MU pre/converter has outputs for proper monitors, so these could be added at a later date.

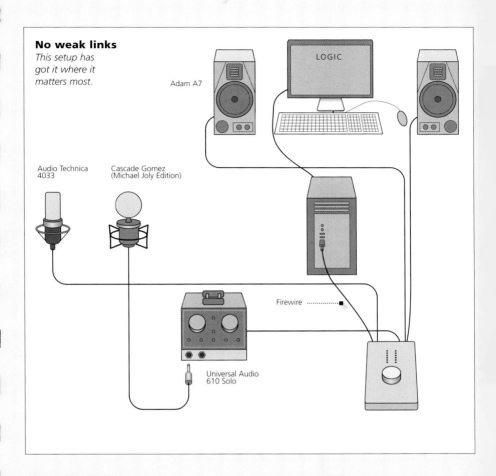

No weak links
This setup has got it where it matters most.

Adam A7

Audio Technica 4033

Cascade Gomez (Michael Joly Edition)

LOGIC

Firewire ·············■

Universal Audio 610 Solo

Budget-conscious

Some readers will baulk at the inclusion of Adam A7 monitors in a budget-conscious setup, a pair of active speakers that could hardly be described as cheap. The point of this setup is to give you an example of a clever configuration that would allow you to achieve truly professional sounding mixes, and that means spending a little more than would be ideal on monitoring—there's no way around it! The 610 Solo is an excellent preamp and DI, but it is listed here as an optional "extra" in the setup because the preamps built into the Duet are more than adequate. The AT4033 and the Gomez are relatively inexpensive mics (a condenser and ribbon respectively), but they are as good as microphones that are much more costly. If you can't produce great mixes with this setup then it's not the equipment's fault!

Expensive

3 If you were given a recording budget from a record company and you intended to record a full drumkit, this would be an excellent setup. With the right acoustic environment, there is no reason why an album could not be recorded and mixed with this equipment to a very high level indeed. Of course, a setup such as this is beyond the reach of a typical home recordist, but we have included it here to give you an example of the sort of configuration into which your home studio might one day evolve. If you check out the secondhand prices of some of this equipment, you might be pleasantly surprised. An AKG 451, Sytek MPX, and Dynamite compressor can all be had for a very reasonable price, and they would all make welcome additions to the smaller setups described here. Some of the other equipment may be more expensive but it still offers tremendous value for money; the SSL X-Desk, Aurora 16, and APS Aeons would certainly fall into this category.

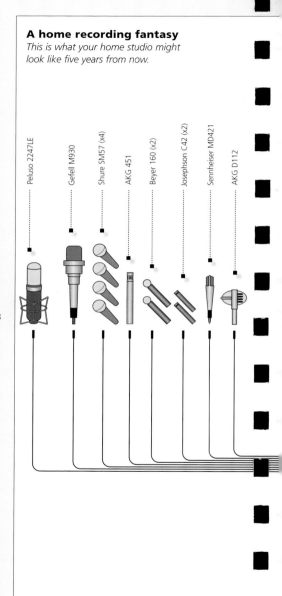

A home recording fantasy
This is what your home studio might look like five years from now.

Peluso 2247LE

Gefell M930

Shure SM57 (x4)

AKG 451

Beyer 160 (x2)

Josephson C42 (x2)

Sennheiser MD421

AKG D112

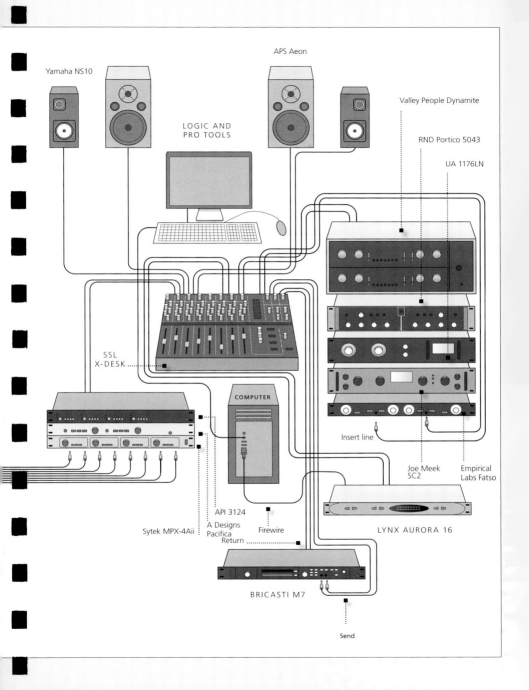

Yamaha NS10

APS Aeon

Valley People Dynamite

LOGIC AND
PRO TOOLS

RND Portico 5043

UA 1176LN

SSL
X-DESK

COMPUTER

Insert line

Joe Meek
SC2

Empirical
Labs Fatso

API 3124

A Designs
Pacifica

Sytek MPX-4Aii

Return

Firewire

LYNX AURORA 16

BRICASTI M7

Send

Chapter 4

Studio setup

 Here you will
see some examples
of what a home studio
setup might look like
alongside some general
advice about how to achieve your
ideal recording space.

Setting up your studio

You've got the equipment, but what's going to live where? How is it all going to connect up, and what stands and furniture do you need? Important questions; a good setup will make recording easier and improve your sound.

Vertical studios floor plan

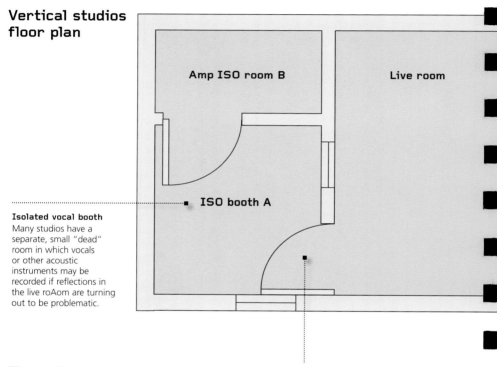

Amp ISO room B

Live room

ISO booth A

Isolated vocal booth
Many studios have a separate, small "dead" room in which vocals or other acoustic instruments may be recorded if reflections in the live roAom are turning out to be problematic.

The traditional studio layout

While you're obviously not working with the same budget as a professional studio, you can get some inspiration from the way they are typically laid out and the "zones" they include. Ultimately, you're doing the same thing as them, just on a more modest scale.

Live room
The live room is the backbone of any studio—it's the place where the sound "happens." Necessary equipment in this room includes microphones to pick up the sound, stands for microphones and sheet music, amplifiers for guitars or keyboards, and headphones for the performers (more on that later). Good live rooms have been acoustically treated to sound "good," usually by eliminating intrusive reflections.

Control room

Every studio has a separate room for the engineer and producer(s) to monitor the tracks as they're recorded. By being sonically isolated from the performer, the engineer can only hear what his recording system is picking up without any interference coming directly from the sound source. This makes equipment adjustment a lot easier as you can clearly hear any changes you're making during a performance. Typically, a triple-glazed window is fitted into the wall between the control room and the live room so that engineer and performer can make eye contact while communicating through the console's talkback facility. The control room houses the bulk of the recording equipment. You'll find most processing and effects units in this room along with the hard disk recorder itself, a computer running Pro Tools or Logic. In high-end studios, there is often a big, expensive console for processing and mixing.

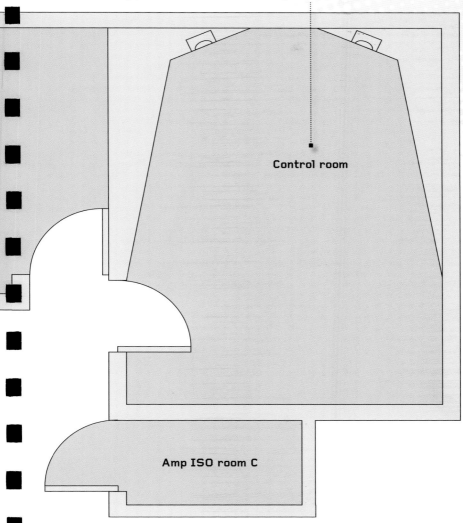

Control room

Amp ISO room C

Home studio layout and function

You might be wondering how studios that sprawl across several rooms relate to your crammed bedroom studio. The reasoning behind having separate rooms, however, applies to everyone.

1 Keep live and monitored sound separate.

You might be lucky enough to have enough room for a separate control room, in which case... go for it! Otherwise, make sure you designate specific areas for performing and engineering. More importantly, never, ever have the monitors playing back your performance as you record unless you're DIing your signal. Otherwise you'll produce a feedback loop as the monitors' output re-enters the microphone and is played back through the monitors again.
If recording equipment and live space are in the same room, engineer and performer must always use headphones to ensure that the monitored sound doesn't leak into the recorded sound.

Essential equipment
Your computer is likely to become the centerpiece of your studio.

2 Keep performance and control areas separate.

If possible, have a special performance "zone" where a player can get comfortable while someone else records. This makes recording easier for all parties involved. If you're on your own, make sure you give yourself space to turn from an engineer into a performer. For example, leave plenty of time between hitting "Record" and singing the first note of your performance. There's nothing worse than rushing from that red button to your microphone, only to bump into your pop shield and knock over the mic stand!

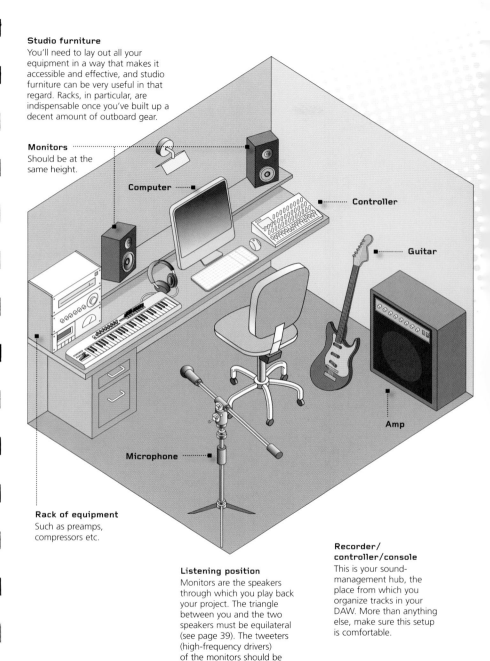

Studio furniture
You'll need to lay out all your equipment in a way that makes it accessible and effective, and studio furniture can be very useful in that regard. Racks, in particular, are indispensable once you've built up a decent amount of outboard gear.

Monitors
Should be at the same height.

Computer

Controller

Guitar

Amp

Microphone

Rack of equipment
Such as preamps, compressors etc.

Listening position
Monitors are the speakers through which you play back your project. The triangle between you and the two speakers must be equilateral (see page 39). The tweeters (high-frequency drivers) of the monitors should be roughly at ear height.

Recorder/ controller/console
This is your sound-management hub, the place from which you organize tracks in your DAW. More than anything else, make sure this setup is comfortable.

Chapter 5

Recording

 The process of recording (or "tracking" as it is sometimes called) can be a lot of fun; but it's also serious business! Before you dive into the fray, threatening helpless instruments with your trusty SM57, arm yourself with some tried and tested methods of recording, from general dos and don'ts to instrument-specific microphone arrangements.

Recording basics

Laying down the tracks for your song can feel like a
vast undertaking, but a pragmatic approach will ensure
a smooth and efficient recording session.

One at a time or all at once?

In a multitrack recording, each
instrument is recorded through
a separate, dedicated input.
For example, you might use one
microphone feeding one input
channel for the voice, three
microphones feeding three channels
for a drumkit, and two microphones
feeding two channels for your
acoustic guitar. These tracks might

HEADPHONE ISSUES

*However your musicians are
being recorded, they'll need to be
wearing a pair of headphones through
which to hear themselves and any
other tracks (live, pre-recorded, or
click track) that they're meant to be in
time with. A good headphone mix can
make a huge difference to the quality
of a performance, as can adjusting the
volume. Singers, for instance, will sing
louder as the headphone mix volume
goes up, or will have intonation issues
if the bass is too quiet.*

end up being heard simultaneously
as a song, but they could be recorded
separately. Multitracking leaves you
with one big decision; do you record
the band members separately,
one track at a time, or do you
have the entire ensemble perform
simultaneously, as they
would on stage?

Scenario: Overdubbing

Overdubbing refers to the
process of recording a track
on top of an existing one, like
adding another layer of detail to a
painting. As with visual art, you start
with the structural elements (the
background) before adding the tracks
that sit "on top" of the foundation tracks
(middleground, then foreground). It is
conventional to start by recording the
drums as they provide the rhythmic
groundwork for all the other parts.
Recording the drums first allows all
subsequent tracks to be played "in
time" with the beat of the song. If
your song contains no drums, choose
whichever instrument provides the
rhythmic backbone of the song. In a
folk song, this might be the strumming
of an acoustic guitar, for example.
The drums are often followed by
bass guitar, which forms a close-
knit background relationship with
the drums. The order in which you
record the middleground tracks such
as rhythm guitars, piano, keyboards,
backing vocals, and incidental

Headphones
*Headphones are an
essential piece of gear
for multitrack recording.*

> "Doubt the conventional wisdom unless you can verify it with reason and experiment."

Steve Albini, legendary production engineer

percussion doesn't really matter, just make sure that they're all done before moving on to the lead vocals and solos that constitute the foreground. These are always left until last to guarantee maximum rhythmic freedom in the performance; a rhythmically solid back- and middleground combined with a relatively free-flowing foreground is what you're after.

Scenario: Recording several players at once

2 You may choose to capture a band playing together. The individual musicians feed off each other to create an enjoyable group dynamic that would be lost if they were recorded separately. Providing you have the space to put several players in your live room and enough microphones, stands, cables, and input channels to record them all, there's nothing to stop you! But as you're using many microphones, be especially aware of phase cancellation (see page 106) and microphones picking up instruments they shouldn't. Use appropriate polar patterns (see page 42) and close-miking to counter this.

Scenario: The best of both worlds

3 The truth is, you'll probably want to mix and match the above techniques as appropriate. You might, for example, record drums separately first, then add a string quartet together before overdubbing bass guitar and lead vocals individually again.

Reality check

Just because you spent all your money on fantasy-island equipment,

Playing together
Recording several musicians playing at once can give your music a lift in terms of vibe and rhythmic feel.

it doesn't mean your music is going to sound great no matter what. The devil's in the detail, and small tweaks to your recording setup can make all the difference. Recording means taking sonic snapshots of the real world, with all its extraneous factors, unpredictability, fuzzy logic, and mutable human nature. Welcome to the world of temperamental humans and volatile acoustic environments! In such a context, being sensitive to the impact of "simple" situations can

make or break a good sound. As a recording engineer, it is essential to be aware of:

• The positioning of instruments, microphones, objects, and barriers in the room: depending on where an instrument, amp, or singer is situated, the reflections off the walls of the studio will vary, imparting a different sonic quality to the recorded track. Objects and acoustic treatment can either create or prevent reflections, so moving them around where possible might improve the properties of the room for your specific recording situation. Most importantly, microphone position is crucial and finding a place where the microphone picks up only the very best of the sound source is a tricky task where small adjustments can make all the difference.

• The mood of the performer. Singers and instrumentalists will perform their best takes when comfortable, focused, and free from distractions. Make sure that the players' headphone mix is right, you don't exhaust them with hundreds of takes in merciless succession, and that there's room for spontaneity and improvisation. Clearing the studio of non-essential personnel is usually a good idea.

• The temperature of the room: make sure, if possible, that players don't get too hot or cold, and that the

MIC PROBLEMS

The biggest issue in miking up any sound source with more than one mic is the risk of phase cancellation, which results in a choked, thin sound. When two near-identical signals are mirror images, they interfere with each other and cancel each other out. Consider an innocent air molecule: One signal is pulling it to the right, the other signal is pulling it with equal force to the left. It ends up not moving at all.

Two signals that mirror each other are said to have "opposite polarity." By inverting the phase of one of the signals, you can usually restore order to your sound and create a situation

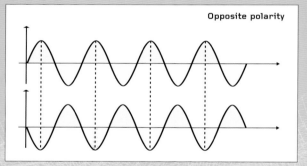

Opposite polarity

where both signals are pulling to the right at the same time.

This is achieved by using the "phase switch," which inverts the voltage of the signal. It should be called a polarity switch (and sometimes it is), but it normally isn't because the problem it fixes is phase cancellation.

^ Two signals that are exact mirror images are polar opposites of each other.

• *So what is phase cancellation? You might have guessed that it's a scenario quite similar to polarity cancellation in that two near-mirror-image signals cancel each other out. If two or more*

temperature is constant. Sound travels more slowly in cold air, changing the acoustic properties of your studio and potentially ruining your setup.

- The state of the instrument. It is vital that the instrument in question (even the human voice) is functioning properly and tuned. There's rarely any point in recording a hoarse voice or an out-of-tune guitar.

A light touch

The above list may make you shiver with responsibility, but thankfully it's usually the tiniest of adjustments that is called for. A singer might just need a glass of water and a ten-minute break; a microphone probably just needs moving three inches to the left; the guitarist's headphone mix might just need turning up a decibel. Many engineers pride themselves in their people skills and minimum fuss when resolving problems. A little flexibility and open-mindedness will get you a long way.

microphones are picking up the same sound source and have near-identical signals, there is always the risk of phase cancellation because the microphones will be receiving the sound at slightly different times. If the difference in time is 180 degrees of the phase of the wave signal, the two signals will look quite similar to the polar opposites shown here (above right), and you'll hear a strange, compromised sound. If phase cancellation is executed perfectly (i.e. inside your DAW, using a plug-in), it will produce silence!

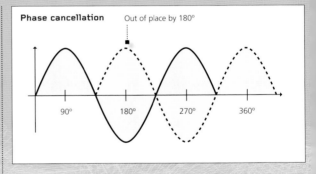

Phase cancellation Out of place by 180°

• So what can be done? You can try the phase switch. Or move one of the microphones farther away or closer to the sound source in order to change the phase difference between the two signals. Most DAWs offer you the facility of introducing a small amount of delay to a recorded track to help

^ When two signals are out of phase by around 180 degrees, they can cancel each other out like polar opposites.

eliminate phase problems. This is not to be confused with delay used as an echo effect. The delay meant here is a way of literally delaying the playback of a track or tracks by a very small amount of time.

Vocals

Unless you're a Mike Oldfield or Steve Vai type of musician, the vocal part of your music is likely to be the most important, so a good recording is absolutely critical.

When you put your producer hat on and begin tracking, you need to be aware both of the technical requirements needed to capture the sound you want and the artistic requirements of the performer. Lose sight of either one of these and your music will suffer, especially if you're capturing a singer's performance. To risk stating the obvious, the voice is unlike other instruments in two important ways; it is responsible for conveying lyrical content and it is part of the performer's body. The most common mistake people make when working with a singer isn't a technical error, it's the mistake of forgetting to make the singer as comfortable as possible. That should be the priority!

Look, no headphones

The mix that is fed into a vocalist's headphones during recording is of vital importance. The next time you are recording vocals, notice the difference in performance that can be invoked by changing the level going into the singer's cans, or even by adjusting the volume of certain instruments in the mix.

However, some singers find headphones intolerable and distracting. The solution is to allow the singer to perform in front of the studio monitors. There is something you can do to help minimize leakage in this situation, a little sound engineer's trick. Once you have finished recording vocal takes, leave the setup exactly as it was and record one more take, this one without the singer. You are effectively recording just the leakage, with the microphone and speakers in the same position as they were. Once you have done this, place the final vocal track and the "pure leakage" track side by side in your DAW and invert the polarity of the latter (see pages 106–107). If you've done it right, phase cancellation should occur and reduce the sound of leakage considerably overall.

Tech talk

The proximity effect
Cardioid pattern mics are usually used for vocal recording, and these are prone to what is known as the "proximity effect," a noticeable rise in bass response when the singer is very close to the microphone. Most of the time you will want to avoid this effect, but sometimes it's just what you're after.

Typical setup
A typical setup for vocal tracking. Note the distance between singer and microphone; any closer and the proximity effect will become noticeable.

RULES FOR RECORDING VOCALS

- The singer should perform while standing. Singing while in a seated position compresses the diaphragm (the singer's, not the microphone's!) which is far from ideal.
- Use a pop filter (see page 41), especially if you are using a condenser mic. Use one of the fine mesh pop shields mounted halfway between microphone and singer. A pop shield will prevent plosives from overloading your microphone and ruining your recording. If you're feeling poor, twist a wire coathanger into a roughly circular shape and secure some stretched nylon pantyhose in two or more layers across the resultant surface area—it makes for an adequate substitute.
- Always supply the singer with refreshment of his or her choice—water, usually—and a convenient place for a lyric sheet and pencil (ideally on a music stand).
- Choose your microphone placement very carefully in relation to the room. Generally, you are aiming to minimize all extraneous noise and reflections, so you might want to put a quilt or some other absorbent material behind the singer and on the floor, or even create an improvised vocal booth. If you find that reflections are a persistent problem, you can also try moving your setup around the room/house/studio until you find the best sound possible.
- Make sure the singer is wearing closed-back headphones that will reduce noise from the headphones "bleeding" into the recording.
- Record everything, from the first warm-up take onward. First takes are often the best, especially when it comes to vocalists.

Acoustic guitar

Whether you're a soulful singer-songwriter or a
wannabe pop diva, a well-recorded acoustic guitar part
can breathe life into your mix like nothing else.

Put that microphone down for a
moment. Before you start recording
you need to take your guitarist on a
little tour of your house/studio, guitar
at the ready. You're looking for the
room, hallway, or landing where the
guitar sounds best. The chances
are that it will be somewhere with
hard floors and a moderately high
ceiling. If just such a location is the
part of your house/studio where you
usually record, great! If not, you need
to seriously consider moving your
recording setup to this guitar-friendly
space and doing your recording

there. It will make a huge difference.
    You could, of course, repeat this
process for every instrument you are
planning to record, so why single
out acoustic guitar in particular?
An acoustic guitar sound will only
really "take off" in a sympathetic
environment, and since an acoustic
guitar is portable, it makes sense
to try out every location you have
access to. Because acoustic guitars
are transient-rich (like drums) yet
also sustained (like pianos), you're
looking for that unlikely place where
the reflections are supportive of both.

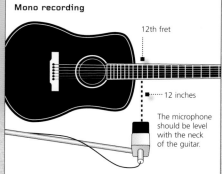

Mono recording

12th fret

12 inches

The microphone
should be level
with the neck
of the guitar.

Recording in mono
Recording an acoustic in
mono is an underrated
technique and it has
the obvious benefit
of avoiding phase
cancellation problems.
The distance between
guitar and microphone
should be reduced if

you are recording in an
unsympathetic room.
A large diaphragm
condenser mic such as
a Brauner Phantom C
would be an excellent
choice.

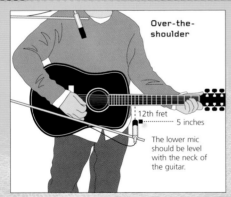

Over-the-shoulder

12th fret
5 inches

The lower mic should be level with the neck of the guitar.

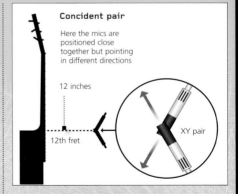

Concident pair

Here the mics are positioned close together but pointing in different directions

12 inches

12th fret

XY pair

Over-the-shoulder mic
Placing a microphone over the performer's shoulder is a good way of picking up what the guitarist hears, and it works well on drums and piano, too. In this case, the "over-the-shoulder" microphone will pick up sound coming from the body of the guitar and the room generally while the mic at the 12th fret captures the thinner sound coming from the fret board.

Coincident pair
Positioning the microphones to form what is known as a coincident or "XY" pair is a great way of getting a sharp stereo image (the two mics should be panned hard left and right) without running into phase problems. You should play around with the position of the pair to achieve the best sound possible, and you should try this with omnidirectional mics as well as cardioids if you are working in a sympathetic room.

Piano

A mainstay of recorded music, the piano is nonetheless one of the most challenging instruments to record.

It is very difficult to advise about the best way to record piano. There are so many miking possibilities and creative decisions to be made… even if we were to list ten different recording setups, you might not find the right one to suit your piano and room. You really need to experiment if you want to capture that dream piano sound!

Recording piano—basic advice

Always make sure the piano you are recording is in tune. Ideally, you should have it tuned before every session.

Open the top of the piano before recording or, if you are recording an upright piano, remove the front panel to expose the hammers and consider removing the kickboard, too.

Try moving the piano away from walls to see if it improves the sound, especially if your piano is an upright. It might be worth putting your piano on a dolly to make the moving process less painful.

Rather than setting up just one pair of mics, set up several pairs in different positions around the piano so that these can be compared quickly to determine the best position.

> **Diaphragm mics**
A pair of small diaphragm condensers such as Josephson C42s and a large-diaphragm mic such as a Gefell UM 92 would be ideal for this arrangement. If you are recording in a spacious room, try a spaced pair of omnidirectional mics positioned 3ft (90 cm) or so away from the piano. As always, watch out for phase problems.

> **Two LDC mics**
Perhaps the most obvious way to mic up an upright, a pair of AKG 414s would suit this arrangement well. For a tight, pop mix you might want to move the mics closer in for a more focused sound, although you will also pick up more mechanical noise from the hammers. Other common methods you should try include stereo pairs positioned several feet away from the piano, either side of the pianist's legs with the kickboard removed, and even behind the piano. And there's no reason you should stick to pairs; a trio of microphones or even one microphone on its own might provide the sound you're looking for.

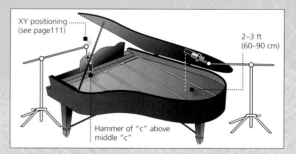

XY positioning
(see page111)

2–3 ft
(60–90 cm)

Hammer of "c" above
middle "c"

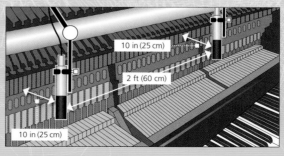

10 in (25 cm)

2 ft (60 cm)

10 in (25 cm)

▶ TOP TIP

Recording keyboards?
A line directly into a
good preamp or DI
will work wonders.
To warm things up,
try saturating the signal
by turning the input on
your preamp/DI up to
its near maximum.
This doesn't always
sound good, but it's
worth a try.

Drums

Along with the piano, a drumkit is the most technically demanding instrument to record and there are a number of potential pitfalls to avoid.

There are loads of prerequisites for getting a great drum sound. You need a well-tuned, decent-to-good drumkit with good-to-excellent cymbals, a good-sounding room, and a good drummer. If you lack one of these things, you might still get an adequate drum sound, but you probably won't be able to achieve a blockbusting, hi-fi, "expensive" drum sound like the ones on your favorite albums.

The good news is that there are loads of options when it comes to miking up and mixing drums, and experimenting with different drum miking setups can be a lot of fun. Here are two typical methods for miking drums.

The Glyn Johns method

Glyn Johns is one of the all-time greats of sound engineering and production with a list of credits that includes Bob Dylan, The Rolling Stones, The Who, and Van Halen. His method of recording drums is famous for providing a big, "live" drum sound using only four microphones—ideal for the home recordist who might not have a big collection of microphones to play with.

Start off by setting up two identical mics that will serve as the overheads. These are responsible for picking up the sound of the kit overall, making up the majority of the drum sound in the mix and providing width in the stereo field.

Experiment with your setup
Don't be afraid to experiment with your drumming setup—something as small as a change of drumsticks might make all the difference.

First overhead

The first overhead is placed directly in front of the drummer on his right-hand side, pointing toward the midway point between toms and snare. During mixing, this overhead should be panned to the right.

Second overhead

The second overhead is on the drummer's far right pointing toward the snare. In order to avoid phase issues, try to position the two overheads at exactly the same distance from the snare, tape measure in hand. During mixing, pan this overhead to the left.

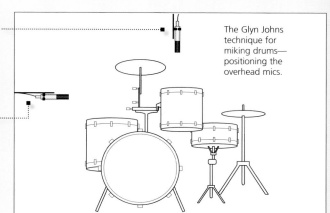

The Glyn Johns technique for miking drums—positioning the overhead mics.

Ribbon microphones, like a pair of ShinyBox or Royer mics, would make ideal overheads for this method. The other two microphones should be positioned to record the snare and kick drum at close range; exactly where and how is up to you. Some people prefer to mic inside the kick drum itself, for example, while others use two kick drum mics, one inside, one outside. The important thing with this method is to position and pan the overheads correctly so that the snare and kick mics can be relatively low in the mix with the overheads doing most of the work.

A typical ten-microphone setup

From the 1970s onward, more elaborate drum miking setups came increasingly into vogue, sometimes involving 15 or 16 mics! The photograph on these pages shows a typical modern drumkit setup.

If you want to set up your drum recording in this way to capture a full, detailed sound, you're going to need a few microphones… Here are some microphone candidates for drumkit duties:

- **Overheads:** AKG 414s/Beyerdynamic M160s/Rode NT-4
- **Toms (x3):** Sennheiser MD421/ Shure SM57/Sennheiser e604
- **Snare (x2):** Shure SM57/ Beyerdynamic M201/Audix i5
- **Hi-hat:** Shure SM57/AKG 451/ Shure SM81
- **Kick:** AKG D112/Audix D6/ Electrovoice RE20
- **Room:** Neumann U87/AKG 414/ Audio Technica 4050SM

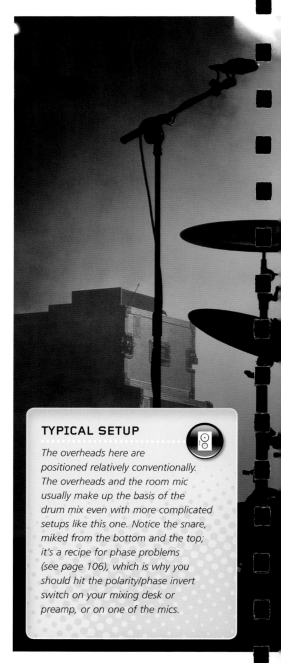

TYPICAL SETUP

The overheads here are positioned relatively conventionally. The overheads and the room mic usually make up the basis of the drum mix even with more complicated setups like this one. Notice the snare, miked from the bottom and the top; it's a recipe for phase problems (see page 106), which is why you should hit the polarity/phase invert switch on your mixing desk or preamp, or on one of the mics.

Electric guitar and bass

Recording amplified instruments is a lot of fun, especially if you have tolerant neighbors!

To begin with, don't get hung up on positioning your microphone when recording a guitar amp. Pay attention to the sound of the amp as you hear it in the room and ask yourself, "Does it sound good?" If you can get a really good tone out of an amp and an in-tune guitar then you're halfway there, and even if you just stick a Shure SM57 in front of the speaker, you'll probably end up with a usable sound.

But you don't just want a decent sound, you want a kick-ass guitar sound. In that case you need to think carefully about microphone selection and placement. A dynamic cardioid mic is a good starting

place, something like an SM57 or Sennheiser MD421. One of these placed about 4 in (10 cm) from the center of the speaker will produce a bright, forward sound; moving the microphone off-center will tend to produce a warmer, balanced sound. You could also try a large-diaphragm condenser mic like a Neumann U87 or Rode NTK, which will produce a brighter, crisper sound overall, or a ribbon mic such as a Beyerdynamic M160 or a Royer 121, which will produce a darker, detailed tone.

Miking an amp
Two or more microphones are often used to record an amp. Each one is recorded to a different track, and these are combined in the mix.

Select your equipment
Having a selection of amps and guitars to choose from will help you to get the sound you're after.

Live vs. recording
Recording a good guitar sound can be quite different from producing a great sound when playing live.

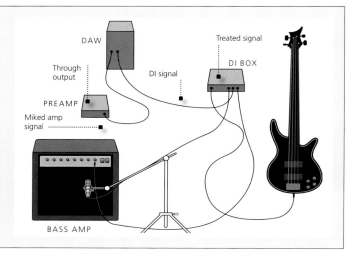

> Conventional/
DI recording

A typical setup to record bass guitar both conventionally and with a DI at the same time. Notice the signal uses the "through" output on the DI. If your DI doesn't have this feature, you may need to invest in a stand-alone signal splitter.

DAW

Treated signal

Through output

DI signal

DI BOX

PREAMP

Miked amp signal

BASS AMP

Bass guitar

There are two golden rules for recording bass guitar. Number one, always use the biggest monitors available when fine-tuning your bass sound, avoiding headphones as much as possible. Headphones, no matter how good they are, cannot reproduce low frequencies with the same accuracy as speakers that actually "move air."

The second golden rule: Always use a DI. The sound of a bass guitar amp miked up with an AKG D112 or MD421 (the usual suspects) can be a tricky thing to get right, and a DIed sound will usually win the day. It's common practice to record bass guitar with a miked amp and a DI simultaneously.

USEFUL TIPS AND TRICKS FOR MIKING AN AMP

When miking up a stack, take care over which speaker you target with the microphone—you might find that one sounds better than the others.

In order to capture more of the room sound, have one microphone (usually a condenser) positioned farther back from the amp, up to 2 ft (60 cm) away. This is an important technique if you want to create a sense of space and "vibe" in your recording.

Very loud guitar amps can damage ribbon mics and even large diaphragm condenser mics, so take care!

Be aware that the "proximity effect" will result in a more bassy sound if you close-mic the amp.

Try moving the amp off the floor by placing it on a chair, for example. This will usually improve the recorded sound overall by reducing interference caused by reflections coming from the floor.

▶❙ **PRO TIP**

In order to keep your recording session moving, make sure you have a supply of spare strings and guitar picks handy. Never rely on your guitarist to look after himself!

Chapter 6

Mixing

 Your ability to make good decisions and listen critically to your own music will be put to the test when the time comes to mix your demo or album. Far too many self-produced recordings are ruined by poor mixing decisions, so you owe it to your music to ensure that your tracks are processed and balanced in a tasteful, professional-sounding way.

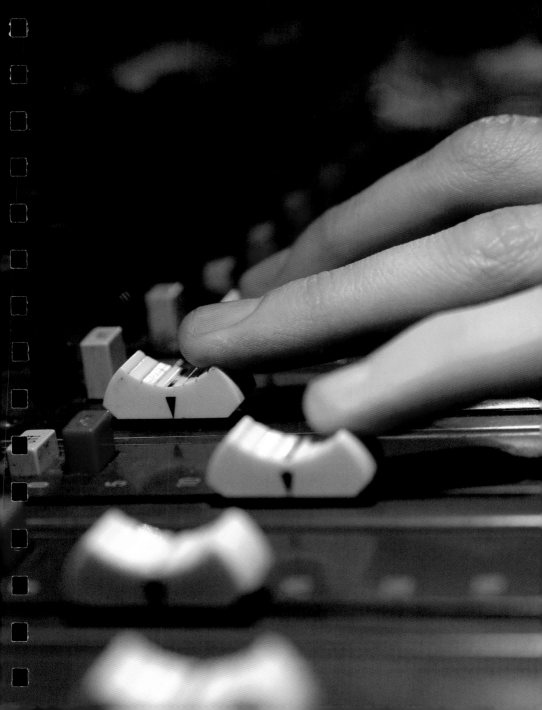

Mixing basics

You've recorded all your tracks, but combine them in playback and they'll sound like a mess. Your song needs to be mixed.

What is mixing?

Mixing is the procedure of combining multiple tracks into a coherent whole. No matter how many tracks your song uses, be it an a capella vocal that only uses three tracks or a complex pop song that uses more than a hundred, these tracks will need to be processed and manipulated in some way before your song sounds like the finished article. At its simplest, this process involves adjusting the levels of the individual tracks until a balanced mix is reached, a mix in which the important instrumental or vocal parts are at just the right level, both in relation to each other and also to less prominent "textural" tracks such as backing vocals. Level adjustments, however, are usually not enough, and there are a myriad of processors and effects available to the mixing engineer to improve the sound of his multitrack recording.

Hands on
A mixing engineer at work, adjusting the levels of individual tracks.

Prepping your tracks

To each track its name
It sounds obvious, but it's useful to assign names to tracks. Label them in your DAW, and stick a long piece of masking tape across the top of your mixing channels if you are using a hardware mixer

and write your track names across it.

Assembling the perfect take
As discussed in the Recording chapter (see pages 102–121), you will have recorded many takes

for each track. You might love, for example, the feel of a particular drum part in a take that's otherwise uninteresting, and want to paste it into another take where the overall performance is better. "Pick and mix" your ⊙

Vintage equipment
The mixing console has been a mainstay of recording studios since the 1960s.

The mixer's arsenal

There are two main devices at your disposal for mixing your recorded tracks: "signal processors" and "effects." Though these terms are often used interchangeably, they describe two distinct operations.

Processors affect the balance of your tracks most dramatically, and they should often be applied before adding effects, which act as mere "decorations" to your mix by comparison.

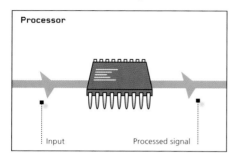

Processor

Input | Processed signal

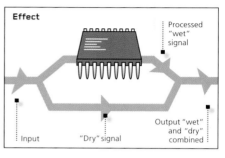

Effect

Processed "wet" signal

Input | "Dry" signal | Output "wet" and "dry" combined

Processor
A processor replaces the original signal with a treated one.

Effect
An effect splits the input signal prior to processing and mixes the altered, "wet" signal with the original, "dry" one, thus adding an extra layer to the original signal.

▶ *favorite bits from each section and combine them into one perfect track. Take time doing this— it's worth it!*

The sound of silence
Acoustically recorded tracks typically contain plenty of isolated noise, such as your vocalist muttering during

⌄ **Software imitates hardware**
DAWs emulate the look and feel of a hardware mixing desk's channel strips.

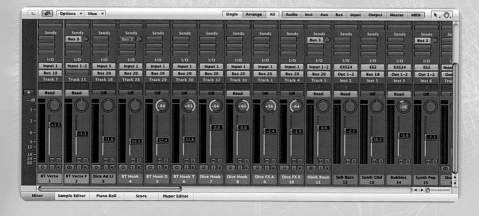

Isolated noise
The guitarist might have been muttering while he recorded his part—one aim of mixing is to eradicate this kind of unwanted sound.

the guitar solo, or the bass guitarist accidentally hitting a string during a two-second pause. Make sure that the track is perfectly silent when it's meant to be by deleting any sound in between performance segments. A noise gate can automatically remove any low-level noise. Persistent background noise during a performance needs to be eliminated with EQ (see page 64).

Tightening the rhythm
You can also correct rhythmic inaccuracies. If the drummer, for example, mistimed an entry and came in early with his crash and kick, you can move it forward in your DAW's track editor until it sounds right. This process can also be automated by a quantizer, which approximates each attack of an instrument to

the nearest MIDI value specified (eighth note, sixteenth note, and so on). In mainstream pop and rock, most background parts (bass, drums, synths, and rhythm guitars) are quantized, which irons out rhythmic unevenness, but can also kill a good performance. Whether you decide to do this depends on how much of your players' musicianship you wish to capture!

Signal processors

You may have guessed by now that compressors and equalizers fall into the category of processors, and their role in mixing is explained on pages 58–61 and 64–67. The first processors you'll want to use, however, are faders.

The fader from a typical mixing desk

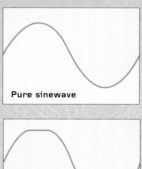

Faders

Faders will determine how prominent you want each track to be in your mix. Together with pan pots and EQ, they make up the most powerful processors in making your tracks sound "good" together. They can be found on virtually every mixing console.

Faders are perhaps the oldest type of signal processor around. Each fader on a mixing desk or software interface acts as a volume control for an individual track that you've recorded. Balancing the levels of your tracks so they sound good together is one of the principal challenges of mixing, and it is the best place to start. Faders used to be rotary dials, but were gradually replaced in the 1960s by the linear sliders that are familiar today. They are the defining feature of a mixing console.

Faders allow you to adjust several track levels at once, and give you an instant overview of where everything's at. In conjunction with the meter bridge, you can see just how loud or "high up" each track is in the mix. Even in the digital age, faders are so highly prized that many engineers purchase hardware interfaces and mixers specifically to be able to use these tactile controls.

CLIPPING

When you are adjusting the signal levels of your tracks, be aware of the maximum capacity of your console or DAW. If you exceed this threshold the signal will start "clipping," distorting the sound in an unpleasant way. Always make sure your signal is within the maximum load of the equipment you're using (be it digital or analog), otherwise it will get clipped.

You can monitor your track's signal levels and how close they are to clipping in the output level display. As the signal gets more powerful, or "hotter," the display's color changes from green, through yellow, to red.

> **Distortion**
Notice how the clipped sinewave has been distorted.

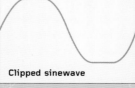

Pure sinewave

Clipped sinewave

Sliding controls

A view across a mixing desk—the sliding faders are simple and intuitive to use.

PANNING

Panning is the way to control the stereo image of your mix. A pan potentiometer (or pan pot) splits your mono signal into two signals (left and right) of variable volumes so you can determine where your track sits in the stereo field with the turn of a knob.

> **Potentiometers (pots)**

On a console, most controls (apart from the fader) are pot knobs.

Compression in the mix

You may know how compression works
in theory, but how and when exactly should
you apply compression in the mix?

If you are recording and mixing music in any popular style, from hip-hop to country to metal, then achieving a professional-sounding product will be impossible without compression. Compression is *the* tool and, next to EQ, it is the form of processing you will find yourself using most. But be careful; over-compression can result in a lifeless, flat mix.

Compression everywhere

At this point you might be asking yourself, "Why is compression so important; surely it's just a form of processing like any other? Surely reducing dynamic range isn't always such a good thing?"

You would be right to ask these questions, and a recording purist would argue that dynamic range should be reproduced faithfully, not compressed. Acoustic, unamplified instruments in a live environment sound so good partly because of their dynamic range, and classical recordings often have no compression applied to them at all. In order to understand why compression is so important to modern music, you need to listen to the classic popular recordings of the 1950s, 1960s, and 1970s, all of which are characterized by the distinctive sound of compression. One of the main things that makes a record sound like a record is compression.

CHANGING SOUND

The sound of records changed during the "golden era" of recording, from the heavy tape compression of old Elvis records to the smooth, transistorized sound of 1970s' Stevie Wonder. Even though it's easier than ever to do away with compression (after all, you don't need to wrestle with multitrack tape machines and vinyl LPs anymore), you might find that an uncompressed mix doesn't sound like it belongs to that tradition of great recordings; that it doesn't sound, well, like a record.

Check out recordings from the 1950s to the 90s to hear the impact of changing recording technology.

▶️ PRO TIP

If you want to apply a generous amount of gain reduction to a prominent vocal or instrumental track, try chaining two or more compressors together. Somehow, having each individual compressor working less hard results in a slicker, cleaner sound than having one compressor pulling out all the stops.

KNOCK-OUT PUNCH 🎧

Above all, percussion instruments and drums in all popular idioms are defined by the use of compression. People often talk about the added "punch" compression can provide. Check out the snare drum sound on Michael Jackson's "Jam," which borders on the ridiculous!

Let's talk quantities

How much compression to use and how often to use it are, above all, questions of genre. If you want your music to have a contemporary rock/metal sound then you will need to compress every track, with unusually heavy compression on drums and vocals. Listen to Soundgarden's classic album *Superunknown*, for example, and you will notice that there is very little dynamic range in the lead singer's performance.

Guitars, even acoustic guitars, get the "smashed" treatment in rock music, too. On System Of A Down's *Steal This Album!* "Roulette" is an excellent example of the use of heavy compression to achieve a full-on rock/metal sound, even within the context of an acoustic guitar-led ballad.

PUMPING

By combining a moderate threshold with a high ratio and a fast to moderate release time, you can achieve another famous compression effect, that of "pumping" or "breathing." This occurs when you can hear the compressor kicking in and kicking out as the signal rises above and drops below the threshold respectively, effectively imparting its own "rhythm" to the track. You will need to play around with the parameters in order to pull this one off, paying particular attention to the threshold. It's worth checking out The Kooks' "Naïve," which uses heavy, pumping compression on its drums very effectively.

Heavy compression isn't merely the preserve of rock music. Fergie's "Big Girls Don't Cry" and Christina Aguilera's "Beautiful" are pop ballads in the traditional sense, yet both feature heavily processed lead vocals with some serious gain reduction smoothing out the singers' performances. However, before you set your vocal track compressor to a "smash" setting (low threshold, high ratio), please pay some attention to the attack and release parameters. Getting these settings right is always important, but nowhere more so than in the application of heavy compression where the compression itself can be more easily "heard."

At the other end of the genre spectrum, a typical low-key singer-songwriter such as Elliott Smith will benefit from a more understated approach to compression with fewer (if any) tracks processed with high-ratio compression.

Parallel universe

Parallel compression is the practice of combining an uncompressed (or lightly compressed) track with a very heavily compressed copy of the same track. Usually, you only need to mix in a little of the "smashed" track to achieve the desired effect. The advantage of parallel compression is that you can combine the best of both worlds—that is, compressed and uncompressed—by adding in the heavily compressed track to taste. To hear parallel compression at work, take a listen to Coldplay's album *Viva la Vida*, on which mix engineer Michael Brauer frequently blends multiple copies of the

▶ PRO TIP

Compression ratios are multiplicative, not additive. This means that if you compress the bass guitar with a ratio of 2:1 when you're tracking and then again at a ratio of 8:1 when you're mixing, you have effectively used a ratio of 16:1 (not 10:1) to compress the bass. Try lowering your ratios in order to avoid a squashed final product!

lead vocal track together, each one processed with a different compressor.

Less sssss

Many compressors have a side-chain input as well as a regular input. When engaged, the signal coming into the side-chain input is the one that will trigger the compressor, while the signal coming into the regular input will be the one acted upon by the compressor. A typical application for this would be to turn the compressor into a "de-esser," a device used to

Modern sound
Tracks by Christina Aguilera often feature heavily processed vocals.

reduce sibilance in a vocal track. To do this you need to send one copy of the vocal track into the regular input and a copy into the side-chain input. The side-chain input copy needs to have its sibilant frequencies (c.5kHz and upward) boosted with an EQ so that sibilance sets off the compressor, applying gain reduction to the other (regular input) copy when sibilance strikes.

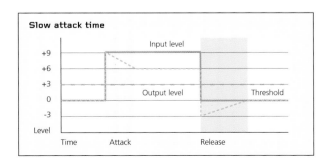

Slow attack time

‹ Slow attack
You can achieve a punchier sound by setting up your compressor with a relatively slow attack time so that the sound is initially "let through" before gain reduction takes place. This has the effect of emphasizing the initial "hit" of the drum, resulting in a punchier, more aggressive sound.

▶ **SEE ALSO** *Equalization* **64** *Mixing basics* **124**

EQ in the mix

Equalization is one of the most powerful tools in music production and mixing, but if used incorrectly it can seriously damage your music's health.

A tale of two EQs

Some sound engineers think of equalization as being either "corrective" or "creative," but it isn't always easy to distinguish between these terms. Corrective EQ usually involves removing problem frequencies from a track; de-essing (see page 133) is a good example of corrective equalization.

Creative equalization, on the other hand, is the process of using EQ to make things sound "as they should"; as they do in your head or as they do on your favorite records. A good example is the way kick drums, snares, and

Corrective EQ
Corrective EQ removes problem frequencies; an example is "de-essing" vocal tracks.

DOS AND DON'TS

Alright, so there are no real dos and don'ts when it comes to making music, but this little list of EQ imperatives might just prove useful.

DON'T *be tempted to rely on a "smiley face" EQ setting too often, if at all. It may seem to provide an easy route to a rounded sound, but it can all too easily lead to an amateurish sounding mix that lacks personality and depth.*

DO *try using the presets that are built into the EQs in your DAW (see page 66). Some of them can be very*

⌄ **Presets**
Example of the "smiley face" EQ setting in Logic.

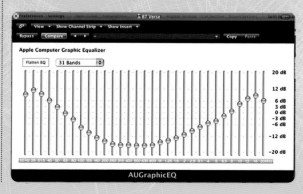

Creative EQ
The drum sound on many records is a result of the use of creative EQ.

▶️ PRO TIP

Here are some other signal processors you might come across:

Auto-tune: A form of pitch-shifting, typically used to fix out-of-tune vocals.

Ring modulator: This effect makes your signal sound buzzy, brittle and bell-like. Think evil robot.

Vocoder: If you've ever heard a "talking synth" on a record and wondered how they got that sound, you're hearing a vocoder.

hi-hats sound on most pop records, which has a lot to do with the use of creative EQ. Kick drums often have a moderate low-frequency boost at around 75Hz and quite an extreme boost between 2kHz and 5kHz, which is effectively a "presence" boost, allowing the kick to be heard more clearly in the mix. If you listen to the kick drum sound on Metallica's *Black Album* you will notice that a substantial amount of high-frequency energy has been EQed in.

Similarly, hi-hats are often subjected to some fairly extreme EQ, with a high-shelf filter boost and a radical roll-off of low and even low–mid frequencies. Snare drums are invariably given some sort of mid-frequency boost—anywhere between 175Hz and 700Hz depending on the song—and you will often hear snare sounds that have been boosted at much higher frequencies and then compressed hard for an aggressive sound that cuts through the mix.

Cut!

What you have just read might have given you the impression that fearless EQing with lots of extreme boosts is the way to go, and in many ways a brave, "Trust your ears!" approach is a very good thing. But there are

⊘ DOS AND DON'TS

effective. There's no shame in frequently using similar settings or presets: some of the world's most famous engineers and producers keep the same settings on their outboard gear from one project to the next! **DON'T** be afraid to experiment by placing EQs at different points in the signal chain (see page 32). For example, try placing an EQ before a compressor (more usually, EQ follows compression), and you should sometimes try placing an EQ before any effects plugins.

DO use high- and low-pass filters. High-pass filters set to around 40–60 Hz get a lot of use in professional recordings, as eliminating unwanted low frequencies will improve your mix overall while clearing the way for instruments such as bass guitar and kick drum. You shouldn't always pass-filter instruments that are not bass-heavy, but there are some instruments such as electric guitar and vocals that nearly always get the HPF treatment. Low-

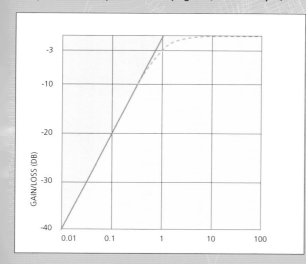

GAIN/LOSS (DB)

-3
-10
-20
-30
-40

0.01   0.1   1   10   100

‹ **High-pass filter graph**
A high-pass filter cuts out the frequencies below its threshold.

also lots of situations where a subtle approach to equalization will yield the best results. Many an old-school sound engineer has been heard to utter the adage, "One cut is better than a hundred boosts," and there are many recording industry professionals who endeavor to rely on a judicious use of cuts rather than boosts when they mix. Bear in mind, also, that not every instrument will respond well to extreme EQ settings. For example, a lead vocal will quickly start to sound unnatural with too much EQ, especially if you are using high Q settings (see page 65).

Vocal distortion
Vocals can sound unnatural with too much EQ.

pass filters are useful too, especially for reverbs, which often have high-frequency content that needs taming for the benefit of the mix. **DON'T** fall into the habit of always soloing a track while you are EQing it. One of the main purposes of using EQ while mixing is to allow "room" for all of the instruments to sit together in the mix by, say, cutting a certain frequency in the keyboard track to give the acoustic guitar track more room to breathe. Some of the best mix engineers rarely engage the solo function on their console for this very reason.

DO bear in mind that EQ is not a panacea. If you are attempting to use EQ to make up for a poorly recorded track then you might find yourself running up against a brick wall. There may be nothing for it other than to re-record the problem track. Alternatively, you could reach for the "mute" button, a solution that is stupidly simple but one that has come to the rescue of many musicians and engineers over the years!

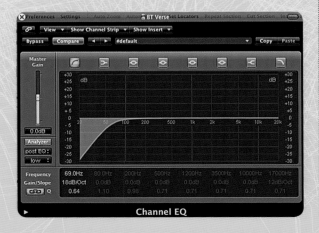

‹ **Software high-pass filter**
A high-pass filter as seen in Logic.

Effects: wet and dry

Adding effects to a recording is like adding spices to your cooking—it's not essential as such, but it certainly makes everything more fun and exciting. But just as too many spices numb your tastebuds, too many effects can make your track sound messy and even silly. A careful, informed addition to the original sound is what's needed.

Reverb—the salt in your mix

Reverb is the most popular effect in music production; it also happens to be the most complex. Reverb simulates the reflections off the walls of an enclosed space by layering an intricate web of "echoes" on top of the input signal. Old-fashioned reverbs don't manage to create the impression of a realistic place. Rather, they imbue a track with a sense of space that can make a song feel bigger and more seductive. Since the late 1970s, more sophisticated reverbs have become available that can accurately mimic the reflective properties of real spaces. Old habits die hard, however, and it is still popular to use distinctly artificial reverbs in music production.

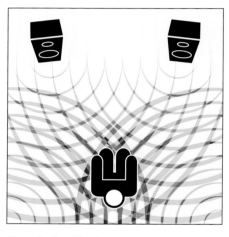

Reverb visualized
Reverb is the phenomenon of many reflections forming a complex addition to the orginal sound.

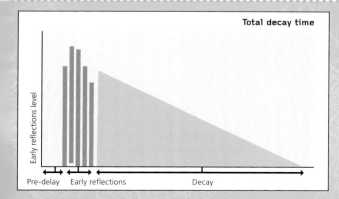

REVERB OVER TIME
Reverb components unfold over time; first the pre-delay, which determines when the reverb starts, and then the early reflections, which are a complex web of distinctive sound echoes whose duration is governed by the decay time.

>> Tech talk

Presets and you

Most processors and effects units, both hardware and software, come with factory presets—settings designed for specific applications or mixing situations. They usually come with enticing titles such as "1960s vintage tape," "Killer Metal Overdrive," "Space Warp," or "Jimi Hendrix." Many home recordists consider these presets a valuable timesaver as it can take ages to configure your compressor or reverb from scratch.

And indeed, presets are a great way to get to know your unit or plugin; just don't use them unquestioningly. Try out as many presets as you can to observe how the designers intended the gear to be used. Then start tweaking parameters and check out the differences—don't be shy, try every knob! In time, you'll probably create your own custom settings that simply "work" for your production.

Artificial flavorings

The problem with naturally occurring reverb is that it is subtle, complex, and difficult to simulate. So hard, in fact, that recording artists frequently seek out the real, homegrown deal over an effects unit: Frank Zappa built his own echo chambers, and Björk recorded an entire album in a cave. Before the advent of digital reverb in the late 1970s, plates or springs in an analog circuit would simulate reverb, resulting in very fake yet pleasing results. With the advent of digital technology came the possibility to mathematically sample and emulate a real environment. These convolution reverbs are, as you would expect,

‹ **Cave effect**
Using digital reverb is a lot easier than recording in a cave!

TYPICAL REVERB PARAMETERS

Pre-delay: *Adjusts the time between the input signal and the first reflection. The longer the time, the larger the space will sound because this is perceived as the time it takes for the sound to travel to a reflective surface and then your ear. It is an easy way to separate the track's transients from the effect if the two sound too intermingled and muddy—good for clarity!*

Diffusion (early reflections diffusion): *Essentially, this factor describes the shape of your simulated room, hall, or spaceship. Is it a giant box, or dome-shaped, or a pyramid? How flat are the surfaces? Perfectly flat surfaces offer little diffusion, as do right angles. The more "organic" a space becomes, the more the diffused and intermingled clearly identifiable echoes become. Low diffusion settings can add presence to long sustained notes, but can* soon sound "jangly" on regular rhythms.

Decay: *This adjusts the overall time the reverb lasts—the longer the decay time, the more cavernous your track will sound. Other reverb events, such as early reflections, affect this "master setting," changing not just the duration but also character and color of the reverb.*

Room size: *This parameter, often measured in imaginary feet, adjusts the overall behavior of*

stunningly realistic. Yet spring and particularly plate reverbs haven't lost their appeal. We've become so accustomed to their artificial sound that digital units and plugins offer simulations, not just of real spaces, but also of analog reverbs.

Plates and springs

These analog methods of creating reverb were originally made of one or more suspended pieces of metal (plates or springs) that vibrate backward and forward in response to the input signal. A pickup similar to that of an electric guitar captured these vibrations and transmitted them to the "wet" output.

Pre-1970s recordings extensively used plate and spring reverbs so strangely, using them today adds a touch of vintage class to

a mix. The unique sound of the more costly and cumbersome plate reverbs is particularly valued to this day—great for vocals and guitars.

Convolution

Convolution uses a mathematical algorithm to replicate a real environment's reverb by convolving a recorded sample of that reverb (generated by a very short, sharp sound) with a new signal (your input). This type of reverb is the most successful at creating the illusion of a real space. It was perhaps overused in 1980s pop, but has since become a tool for recreating a subtle, realistic sensation of space.

a room according to its size by altering the time between reflections.

Damping/hi-cut:

In natural environments, certain materials (such as stage curtains) absorb high frequencies, while reflecting lower ones. This parameter gives you control over whether your track sounds like it's being performed in, say, a padded cell (cloth walls) or an elevator (metal walls and mirrors). The "material" of your imaginary walls can be adjusted with the

degree of high frequency damping, which takes the shape of a low-pass filter with an adjustable cut-off frequency. Often, high-pass

filters are on offer too, and some reverbs offer a more complex shelving EQ to adjust the reflections' frequency response.

Delay

In some ways, delay is like a really primitive reverb. Instead of a complex plethora of echoes, a delay unit offers only a few distinct echoes, and modern delay units offer panning, filter, and volume controls over each of those distinct echoes. Delay is used a lot in today's music, especially on vocals where carefully configured delays are used in combination with reverbs to give the effect of spaciousness. Check out Beyonce's "If I Were a Boy" for a typical contemporary delay effect on lead vocals.

Used more traditionally, delay can give your track a dragging, searching, even disoriented feel: Think John Lennon, who loved the effect on everything from vocals to drums. However, it is quite popular to set the delay times in time with the tempo of the song for a denser rhythmic texture or polyphonic

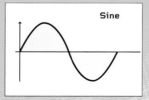 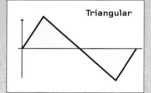

imitation of individual notes or even entire sections of music. Queen's Brian May loves to use this sort of delay on his guitar solos, for example.

Modulation effects

This group of effects is essentially an extension of delay, but is crucially different in two ways:

1) The delay times are very short (no more than 30 milliseconds) so the ear perceives the input and the delay as one signal. Such close delays create peaks and troughs in the output's frequency response as the two signals interfere with each other—this is known as a comb filter.

2) The delay time is varied over time to make the comb filter sweep across the frequency response. A user-definable LFO (low-frequency oscillator) typically governs this fluctuation, which creates the modulation these effects are named after.

Flanging

Flanging is historically the oldest modulation effect, and was allegedly invented during the Beatles' recording sessions for *Revolver*. It involved two synchronized tape recorders playing an identical track and being recorded. An engineer would place his finger on the rim of one of the tape reels (the flange),

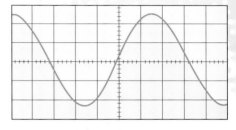

Comb filter
The peaks and troughs resemble the notches in a comb—effectively a shifting, shelving EQ. Depending on the effect, they can be evenly or irregularly spaced.

Speed/rate: *This determines the frequency at which the LFO shape recurs, usually only a few Hertz. A higher speed brings about a more aggressive modulation, sounding increasingly "buzzy."*

Sweep depth: *This controls how much the delay time actually changes (the amplitude of the LFO), and is measured in milliseconds. Again, a great depth means greater pitch modulation and a more "out-of-tune" feel.*

Chorus effect
The chorus effect takes it name from the phenomenon of hearing a choir.

causing that track to speed up and slow down. These days, an LFO takes the place of the engineer's finger.

The resulting mix has been variously described as "whooshing," "swooshing," "swirling," and "swooping" as the two tracks modulate. This effect is delicious on rhythm instruments, especially guitar and piano, where it is most commonly used today.

Chorus
Chorus is named after the effect of hearing a choir—many voices performing the same music, yet all at very slightly different pitches, different timbres, and at different times. The ear perceives these modulating voices as one grand voice coated in a shimmering gloss. The chorus effect emulates this by creating one or more short delays with fluctuating delay times controlled by an LFO. Sound familiar? It is! The only real difference between chorus and flanging is the delay time involved: up to 20 milliseconds counts as flanging,

more than that as chorusing.

Also, a traditional flanger uses only one delay, whereas a chorus uses several. These create the impression of multiple performers, and the variable delay time modulates the pitch of these "extra" voices to create the illusion of slightly and variably out-of-tune instrumentalists or singers. It is popular on lead instruments such as vocals and lead guitars, but will lend richness and depth to most parts. However, as with all effects, it is best used sparingly for the majority of applications.

Multiple vocalists
Even if you have only one vocalist, you can create the effect of more voices using the chorus effect.

"spacier" sound.

The phaser sounds more otherworldly than its predecessor, the flanger. It was hugely popular when first introduced in the 1970s, when bands like Led Zeppelin used it on everything from guitars to drums ("Kashmir" is a great example).

Phase shifters (phasers)

This effect sounds quite similar to a flanger, but it is created in a very different way, originally using an electrical circuit to shift the phases of the input rather than using a tape delay. Phase shift (or delay time) depends on the input frequency, so the resulting comb filter is irregularly spaced, which lends the phaser its unique, slightly deranged character. The phase shifts occur in stages, and analog phasers come in four-, eight-, and 12-stage models while digital phasers have been known to have as many as 32 stages. This affects the number of notches in the comb filter; for every two phaser stages, one notch is added. For example, a 12-stage phaser has six notches. As you'd expect, higher-stage phasers have a richer and

Mixing mistakes

Mixing is a real art-form that takes years of experience to perfect. If you are about to mix for the first time or if you've only done a few mixes before, it's probable that you won't be able to achieve a completely convincing, professional-sounding, well-balanced mix. But don't despair! This section of the book is here to point you in the right direction and stop you making some common mixing mistakes.

Common mixing mistake #1: The order of work

Different mix engineers have different ways of starting a mix. Some engineers throw up all the faders and make adjustments until a rough balance is achieved before commencing "proper" mixing. Others start with the drums, getting a balance between snare, kick, and cymbals before adding the bass and then building the mix up track by track. Some engineers (such as Geoff Emerick of Beatles fame) will even mix an entire song without the kick drum and bass tracks, whose low-frequency energy can be distracting; bass and kick are added to the mix last.

While there are no strict rules about how you should commence work and the order in which you should do things, there are some things you should do "in order." For example, if you intend to apply compression to the mix bus then you should do this at the start of your mixing session, because mix bus processing will affect everything else you do. In general, you should try to get the boring, administrative side of mixing done first, like making sure all your tracks are clearly labeled (whether on your mixing console or inside your DAW), your best takes are chosen, and all your analog auxiliary sends and inserts are set up and ready to go. Oh, and before you dive into a mix and start EQing and compressing, make sure you pay some attention to panning. Cleverly panned instruments will often have their own "place" in a mix without the need for EQ or effects.

Common mixing mistake #2: ITB gain staging

Gain staging is an important consideration when you are processing signals in the analog domain (see page 34), but poor ITB gain staging is a commonly overlooked problem. Obviously, you need to watch out for the red "clipping" indicators on your DAW's faders, both individual track faders and the master fader. You need to watch your plugins, which can also be clipped—a problem that can be fixed by reducing the plugin's input

SHOULD I BE DOING THIS MYSELF?

That's a very good question, especially if you are talking about a song you hope will be played on the radio, or a complete, professional-sounding album. For the purposes of a demo, the cost of having your recording mixed by an engineer at your local studio might be prohibitive; after all, the purpose of a demo is to show off your musical/songwriting talent, not your skills as a producer. But if you haven't done much mixing before and you are hoping to produce work of commercial quality, then it might be worth contacting your local studio and finding out how much it would cost to have someone do your mixing, or ask if you can sit in on a session and watch a professional at work.

level or placing a gain plugin before the problematic "clipping" plugin in the signal chain. Bear in mind that the gain staging of each channel needs to be monitored constantly as you mix because any change in fader level, for example, will have a knock-on effect later in the signal chain.

ITB clipping isn't always audible to the novice mix engineer, and in the context of a heavily distorted rock song there's a chance that it won't matter much. All the same, it is good practice to avoid clipping at all costs and leave quite a bit of headroom on the master fader for the benefit of the mastering engineer—even if that mastering engineer is you! (See Introduction to mastering, page 152.)

Common mixing mistake #3: Making everything louder

Most of the time, things sound better when they're louder, and this applies to individual tracks in a mix as much as anything. The classic beginner's mistake is to push the snare fader up... yeah, that sounds cool. But wait, the bass guitar isn't prominent enough, so the bass guitar fader goes up too, followed by the keys, vocals, and so on. You can see where this is going; the beginner ends up with exactly the same mix he had earlier, only now everything's 4dB louder! The easiest way to avoid this problem is to be aware of the possibility of it happening. But if you still find yourself falling into the trap, try pulling all the faders down a little and turning your monitors up to a point at which they are almost too loud. By doing this you will probably find yourself leaving the faders alone, or even pulling faders down.

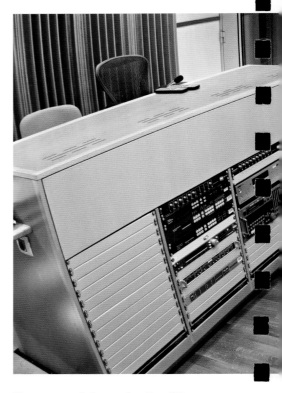

Common mixing mistake #4: Using your eyes

The shiny graphics in your DAW look great, and every mixing decision you make has a cool visual representation. ITB equalizers, for example, allow you to "see" the frequencies you have boosted or cut. In some ways, it's great that things can be visualized, as long as you remember that you are trying to achieve sonic perfection. It is far too easy to get carried away with what you can see, and sometimes people shy away from an extreme bit of EQ or automation because it looks wrong. While mixing, try turning the computer monitor off every now and

again, and keep the lighting subdued. Relaxing your eyes can make more of a difference than you would imagine.

Common mixing mistake #5: Not knowing when to stop

Like any process of artistic refinement, mixing a demo or album can go on and on and on, undergoing revision after revision. If you mix without time constraints, you might end up obsessing about minute details that are just not important enough to warrant hours of consideration, and as soon as you feel yourself start to go backward with a mix, it might be time to stop.

Having said this, it is also important to save your progress as you mix so that you can always "go back" to a decent rough mix if things start to go downhill. The "Save As…" function is your friend, and the great mix engineers such as Jack Joseph Puig and Michael Brauer are all in the habit of saving preliminary mixes as they work.

Chapter 7

Mastering

To get the most from your recording you will need to master it. Whether you intend to master your own music or employ a mastering engineer to do it for you, you'll need to understand what mastering is and how it can help your music.

● **SEE ALSO** *Recording basics* **102** *Mixing basics* **124**

Introduction to mastering

Mastering is the process of getting your music into your chosen medium, such as CD or MP3, while maintaining the highest audio quality possible. It sounds simple, but there's more to it than you might think.

If the history of recorded music was erased forever, and the tradition of recording music began today with today's technology, the need for such a thing as a dedicated mastering engineer would be in doubt. After all, there is software built into every modern DAW that allows you to master your music, applying a final layer of compression and EQ to the left and right channels and finalizing everything as a CD or computer file. Despite this, nearly every commercially released album or single has been mastered in a dedicated mastering suite by a professional mastering engineer. So what's going on?

Ready for consumption
Mastering can improve a song's suitability for MP3 players and iPods.

LOUDNESS WARS

You may have noticed during mixing that things usually sound better when they're louder, and there is immense pressure from record companies to make albums sound as loud as possible. Their reasoning is that a louder song will stand out from the competition when played on the radio, your sound system, or computer speakers. However, all sound reproduction systems have a fixed maximum amplitude beyond which they cannot be pushed. The mastering engineer is tasked with increasing perceived loudness, and this is achieved by a number of processes including aggressive limiting and compression. The result is a louder-sounding but relatively lifeless final product. As you would imagine, everyone who cares about audio quality is upset about this trend, and even the mainstream media has taken notice. Recently, articles have appeared in major newspapers and music magazines about the ever-decreasing dynamic range of commercial releases.

Playback

*Methods of playback
are continually changing;
mastering engineers need
to tailor music to the
media that will eventually
store and reproduce it.*

Mastering vinyl

If you were to travel back in time, the
necessity of a dedicated mastering
engineer would become obvious. The
most important medium in the history
of recorded music was vinyl, and
the process of cutting a vinyl master
disk was—and is—very far from
straightforward. There are a number
of technical difficulties involved
in mastering to vinyl, and it was
certainly a process that demanded a
specialist's knowledge.

By the late 1970s, awareness of the
aesthetic component of the mastering
process had grown to such a degree
that some mastering engineers were
renowned for the qualities they would
bring to a recording. The promise
of better stereo imaging, improved
balance of frequencies, separation
of parts, and definition of transients
made the mastering process an
essential tool in the production of
commercially competitive records.
When CDs arrived, mastering
engineers continued to use specialist
equipment to improve the quality of
recordings and apply a final "gloss"
to the production.

What a mastering engineer does

If a mastering engineer is provided with a collection of songs that will constitute an album, one of his jobs will be to ensure that the whole album is sonically coherent. He will manage the levels so that one song is not too much louder than its neighbors, for example, and he will make sure the correct amount of time elapses between each song. If there are any glitches or problems that were not sorted out at the mixing stage, the mastering engineer will use specialist software to remove them, or at least make them less noticeable.

By using a combination of EQ, limiting, compression, and multi-band compression, the mastering engineer will enhance the sound of an album, bringing it closer to the tonal balance and loudness of other commercially successful albums of the same genre. Multi-band compression is a sort of frequency-conscious compression in which some frequencies are compressed more than others. If the mastering engineer spotted a kick drum in need of more dynamic control, he could apply more compression to lower frequencies without affecting the rest of the mix.

Do I need a mastering engineer?

If you are producing a demo, the short answer is "no." The purpose of a demo is to showcase your talent as a composer and performer, not your ability to produce something that sounds completely finished. The mastering EQ and compression presets available in any DAW are more than adequate for finalizing a demo.

If you are intending to release something commercially, establish your own record company, or produce a whole album yourself, taking your music to a reputable mastering engineer is advisable. A dedicated mastering suite will have superb acoustics, monitoring, converters, and outboard. Make sure you are able to attend the session to communicate your wishes to the mastering engineer, and your music will certainly benefit.

One of the bonuses of taking your music to a mastering engineer is the feedback he will be able to give you about the quality of your mix. There is a possibility he will even send you away to remix your music if he feels there are too many problems for him to fix! For this reason, always try to get your music sounding as good as it can before you send it to be mastered. It is a common mistake to assume a mastering engineer will be able to miraculously reverse poor recording and mixing decisions.

What should I bring?

Communicate with your chosen mastering engineer before your

session so you know what to expect and how to deliver your files. It would be typical to provide a single stereo ".wav" file for each song, but some mastering engineers prefer stems, which means you would need to provide perhaps three or four stereo ".wav" files, sub-grouping different elements from each song into their own stem. For example, your mastering engineer might prefer to have bass guitar and drum tracks in one stem, effects in another and all other instruments in stem number three.

You should expect your mastering engineer to offer services beyond the initial session. A good engineer will send you home with a master and allow you to live with it for a few days, giving you a chance to play it through domestic sound systems and make sure you're happy with it. If there's anything you want to change, a good mastering engineer will then change it and generally ensure that you are satisfied with the result.

The finished article
Fully mastered CDs, packaged and ready to be sold, along with promotional material, from UK band The Kaves.

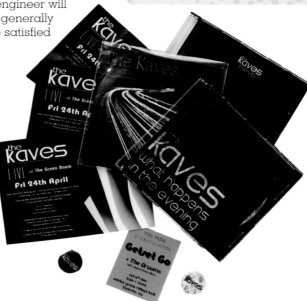

Chapter 8

Getting it on the web

Exploiting the marketing potential of the internet is compulsory if you're an ambitious musician. The guide to doing this on the following pages will help you to get your music heard by as many people as possible.

Social networking websites

You're probably familiar with the concept of social networking services on the internet—online communities whose members share their thoughts and interests with each other.

Unlike message boards or forums, social networking sites format sharing and self-exhibition into a user-defined, interactive web page unique to each member; this is known as a profile. Members can view each other's profiles, exchange private or public messages, post in each others' "Comments" sections, and become "friends" (though strangely not "enemies"!).

Practically all bands and solo artists use these sites to get their music heard, and a select few even manage to achieve fame and fortune as a result. Both the Arctic Monkeys and Calvin Harris, for example, apparently got record deals out of their MySpace presences. Indeed, as MySpace.com is perhaps the oldest social networking site used

to promote new music, it provides an essential internet presence you simply can't afford to miss out on. An artist or act without a MySpace page is like a film without a trailer, so you need to get yours up and running as soon as possible.

MySpace rules

MySpace is the first and most popular social networking site for musicians, so this discussion is centered on setting up social network profiles around it. Subsequent network sites have adopted similar principles so you can easily transfer your MySpace skills to other networking sites once you've got the hang of things. Other major social networks are listed on page 160.

MYSPACE 101

Here are some guidelines to get you started: Sign up specifically as a musician, otherwise you won't have the option of uploading MP3s for visitors to listen to. When registering, choose a MySpace URL that hasn't been taken; one bearing at least a vague resemblance to your band name. You'd be surprised at how many acts' URLs don't correspond to their name.

You can upload four tracks for free, and that's all you really need. As with a demo, choose the tracks that best represent you. If you like, you can set your page to always start with your catchiest "single-material" song.

The best way to network is to request friendships from other members— musicians and non-musicians alike. That way, people will visit your site and listen to at least ten seconds of your music while they examine the essentials of your page, which is just one reason why it's good to have

Load your profile

A no-frills, un-tweaked profile page will instantly bore those who visit your profile. Customizing your page is not optional—you'll find few MySpace music pages that haven't been altered from the classic blue-on-white look. Most social networking sites can be customized, the method varying from site to site. There are many websites that tell you how to do this and offer code for you to paste to change your page's look.

your "best" song playing. If you get on well enough with your new "friends," you might include each other in your favorites list, which will increase your exposure.

The more there is to look at on your page, the longer people will linger, and the more music they will inadvertently listen to. Make your page colorful,

image-laden, and write an entertaining biography! Promote your stuff on other profiles' comments section—everybody does it. Update your page regularly. Keep the community posted on new releases, gigs, or other developments.

To get the most out of any social networking, you need to put in the hours.

That means logging on every day, making new friends, leaving comments, chatting, and finding out about other musical acts. Giving admiration to other musicians is considered good etiquette, and who knows? You might meet the collaborator of your dreams.

► **SEE ALSO** *Band name and image* **22**

The most important sites for you

Here some of the major social networking sites are compared. They each have their strengths, and which site you use will depend on your material and the kind of audience you hope to reach.

SITE	HOW IS IT USEFUL?	SPECIAL FEATURES
MySpace	*The standard website for musicians. Allows you to upload up to four tracks, images, biography, and upcoming gigs.*	> *The original website for sharing music and meeting other musicians* > *Create your own personalized URL*
YouTube	*The best networking website for hosting and sharing videos. Allows you to create your own channel through which you can distribute video material. Supports web widgets (known as players), which means you can place your video on other websites such as MySpace. Indispensable if you have any video material.*	> *Upload videos* > *Create your own channel* > *Renowned worldwide*
Facebook	*Supports neither music nor video directly, but is the most interconnected, communicative network. In comparison, other networks can get a bit lonely at times. Perfect for setting up fan clubs and mail lists.*	> *Huge network of contacts, including non-musicians* > *Instantly interactive*
Bebo	*Similar to MySpace, but with a few interesting deviations. All band members, for example, sign up separately as musicians before forming a band. This way, if your band breaks up, your social networking contacts and friends aren't lost as a result—and you might even form a new act with one!*	> *"What's Hot: and "Best of Bebo"* > *Upload your own videos and music*

Note

The world of social networking websites is an ever-changing landscape, and a comprehensive list of relevant sites for promoting your music would be out-of-date in no time. Use your instincts as a web user in determining which new up-and-coming sites might be of use to you, and ask your friends how they find out about—and follow—new music.

WHAT CAN I CUSTOMIZE?	USERS
Pretty much everything: backgrounds, color schemes, layout, fonts, border types, you name it… To do so, you need to enter HTML and CSS code into your biography. Countless free websites host generators to help you with this; you fill out a form with the changes you want and it generates code for you to cut and paste into the biography section of your profile. Just enter "customize myspace" into a search engine.	*> Musicians* *> Music fans* *> Also many non-musicians*
You can customize both your channel and the player widget. No computer code required—YouTube allows you to do it from the comfort of menus and forms. Just go to "Edit Channel" to change your channel's look, or to "Custom Video Players" for creating your own player.	*> Anyone and everyone, including musicians*
Customization not possible.	*> Anyone and everyone, including musicians*
You can download Bebo skins from many websites. Just search for "bebo skins."	*> Musicians and celebrities* *> Fans* *> Also many non-musicians*

● **SEE ALSO** *Band name and image* **22**

Your own website

If you're serious about your internet presence, profiles on networking sites won't be enough. You'll also need a dedicated space to convey your message and style.

For many unsigned acts, a MySpace page is sufficient, because music, photos, and upcoming gigs can all be uploaded there. And yes, setting up your own website does involve a bit of work. Your own website will, however, give more meaning and presence to your self-promotion. If you've got a really cool and unique website you instantly "taste" better and appear more convincing. Sad but true.

Domain name

A domain name is the URL that you would type into an internet browser to access your site, for example, "www.yourbeautifulsite.com." Hopefully, you have a band name at this point (see page 22) that you can base your domain name on. Get inspiration for names and variations from other acts whose website address appears on their MySpace page. You can find out easily whether your ideal URL is taken or not by accessing it on the internet. If it takes you to an existing website, you'll have to tweak your domain name until you've come up with one that's available.

Web-hosting services

Web-hosting services allow you to upload your site onto their servers so that anyone with an internet connection can access them. They can also register domain names on your behalf, and even supply you with basic tools to construct your website. To keep things simple, register your domain name through the web-host service provider you'll be using. There are many providers out there, so check them out online, comparing the quality of service and the fees of the competing providers.

VARIATIONS

Imagine you're looking for a domain name for your band, the Crazy Elephants... If, say, "thecrazyelephants.com" is already taken, you could try:

1. *Other suffixes such as thecrazyelephants.co.uk, thecrazyelephants.org, thecrazyelephants.net, and so on.*

2. *Acronyms such as "tce.com."*

3. *Add "band," "music," or "web" to the domain. For example, "thecrazyelephantsmusic.com", "tceband.net," and so on.*

4. *Add hyphens, e.g. "the-crazy-elephants.com."*

5. *Or just go with something that relates to your band name like "elephantcraze.com" or "tramplingthesavannah.com."*

Anatomy of your site

An examination of the various mark-up and scripting languages used to build websites is a whole other book in itself. But whichever way you choose to create your pages, whether it's in code, with software such as Dreamweaver, or with an online website builder, you must be sure not to lose sight of the following:

Cool stuff

Why not intersperse the strictly musical pages of your site with political commentary, eco-activism, a gallery of weird and wonderful photos, poems, reviews… the list is endless, and it will all help to get people's attention and give your music the exposure it deserves.

Music

Have some of your material available to listen to. This can be directly through your site, or via a MySpace link. If possible, have a song running in the background while visitors navigate the site so they will be listening to your music while taking in your visuals. You need to hit them with a comprehensive impression of your act all in one go.

Blog

Let visitors see a more personal, intimate side of you, the artist(s). You could describe a bad day at the studio or a great gig; any seemingly mundane topic will grab people's attention if it appears real and sincere.

Mailing lists

Keep your fans and any interested folk up to date with changes to the website.

Promotional photos

You'll need a special gallery for photos from shoots and gigs. These are crucial for giving visitors a flavor of the lifestyle or ethos you wish to convey. Post your own music video if you have one.

News

Each event should come with a press release, be it a new album, a new band member, upcoming shows and events, or even a band split. Make sure any "hot-off-the-press" news is on your main page.

Chapter 9

Playlists

Here is a list of outstanding recordings that will inspire and educate you. Listen to these albums on the best speakers you have available in order to appreciate the sound engineering skill and production brilliance that is on show.

Bob Dylan
Bob Dylan performing live.

Playlists

24 albums from a range of genres, selected for the sound-engineering skill and production brilliance that they display.

10,000 Days/Tool (2006)

Produced by: Tool
Engineer: Joe Barresi

For many, modern metal has become a sterile affair, with quantized drums and predictable rectified guitar tones. *10,000 Days* is different because Tool are a group of ambitious, skilled musicians who have found a perfect foil in Joe Barresi. Barresi does a superb job of engineering and mixing the album. The sound is rich, with well-mixed bass frequencies and a level of compression that keeps things aggressive without detracting from the shifts in texture that occur throughout the album.

Key track
Check out the opening track and single, "Vicarious".

Abbey Road/The Beatles (1969)

Produced by:
George Martin
Engineer: Geoff Emerick

As the last Beatles album to be recorded, *Abbey Road* benefited from what was state-of-the-art recording equipment at the time. It was recorded on an eight-track tape machine (previous albums had used four-track recording) through a new sort of mixing desk that dispensed with tubes in favor of solid-state technology. There is a wonderfully evocative quality to the sound of this album, one that today's engineers continue to emulate whenever a "retro" vibe is called for.

Blood On The Tracks/ Bob Dylan (1975)

Produced by: Bob Dylan
Engineer: Phil Ramone

It is difficult to credit a single engineer or producer for this album. It was recorded in two sessions with different personnel, one in New York and one in Minneapolis. That Dylan's best album resulted from

such a troubled production process is somewhat surprising; nonetheless, this remains a crucial reference-point for singer-songwriters everywhere.

Continuum/John Mayer (2006)

Produced by: John Mayer and Steve Jordan
Engineers: various

If you are looking for the epitome of impeccable modern production and mixing, this is it. Some may find the lush production values of this album a little off-putting, so if you like your music gritty and raw, look away now! But as a technical example of just how expensive-sounding things can get, check this one out.

Key tracks
At the very least, the songs "Gravity" and "Vultures" are worth a listen.

Dark Side Of The Moon/Pink Floyd (1973)

Produced by: Pink Floyd and Alan Parsons
Engineer: Alan Parsons

This definitive prog-rock album is full of innovative production techniques and special effects. Alan Parsons also engineered on *Abbey Road* and he triumphs as engineer/producer of this ambitious concept album.

Endtroducing/DJ Shadow (1996)
Produced and engineered by: DJ Shadow

For anyone interested in pop, hip-hop, or drum machines, this is essential listening. The entire album was produced on an Akai MPC 60 drum machine and it really is a masterclass in how to make music using nothing but samples and drum loops. If you want to hear the "next step" in the evolution of sample-centric music, try *Since I Left You* by The Avalanches.

The Eraser/Thom Yorke (2006)
Produced by: Nigel Godrich
Engineer: Graeme Stewart

Few (if any) producers bring a signature sound to every project they are involved with the way Nigel Godrich does. Any Radiohead album from the last 12 years would have a place in this playlist, but it is Radiohead frontman Thom Yorke's solo album that best represents Godrich's virtuosic production and engineering ability. Samples, synths, and sublime distortion abound, along with Yorke's sometimes unconventional but always well-judged vocal performances.

Fear Of A Black Planet/Public Enemy (1990)
Produced by: The Bomb Squad
Engineers: various

This witty, energetic album should be one of your key reference disks if you're producing rap, hip-hop, or any sort of music that uses samples heavily.
Key track
"911 Is A Joke" is one of the stand-out songs on this album; it manages to evoke the spirit of 1989, which is no mean feat!

Figure 8/Elliott Smith (2000)
Produced and engineered by: Tom Rothrock, Rob Schnapf, and Elliott Smith

Smith is often thought of as a singer-songwriter, but he appears here as an exponent of full-on, elaborate indie rock. The songwriting and arrangements are superb, while the production is intelligent; intricate without being overly ornate. There has never been an indie act with anything like Smith's musical ability, and it is difficult to think of another record company-produced album of the last 25 years with the compositional complexity of *Figure 8*.

Hotel California/The Eagles (1976)
Produced by: Bill Szymczyk
Engineers: various

Those who record music often claim to be after a "warm sound." It is difficult to think of a warmer-sounding album than this one. In fact, many engineers and producers have been known to put this album on a pedestal for its sonic qualities—and rightly so! This album really does have a beautiful sound with the magic combination of each instrument sounding full and rich in its own right while also having its own "place" in the mix.
Key track
Warning: If you listen to the title track through good monitors you may be left with no alternative but to go straight out and buy a multitrack tape machine!

Houses Of The Holy/Led Zeppelin (1973)
Produced by: Jimmy Page
Engineer: Eddie Kramer

Zeppelin's fifth album departs from the stripped down blues/rockiness of their earlier output, exploring a greater diversity of style and texture. Page is a producer at the top of his game here, and his collaboration with Zeppelin mainstay Eddie Kramer (who also engineered Jimi Hendrix and AC/DC, among others) results in a fantastic-sounding album. Great guitar tones, and a great drummer.

In Utero/Nirvana (1993)
Produced and engineered by: Steve Albini

It is well known that Nirvana were unhappy with the sound of their breakthrough album *Nevermind*. A desire to achieve a raw, honest sound with what was to be their final studio album brought them to Steve Albini, an engineer with a distinctive approach to recording and mixing. Albini brings an aesthetic of uncompromising authenticity to his productions, eschewing the ubiquitous "fix it in the mix" approach shared by the vast majority of those in the music industry.
Key track
Listen to the song "Milk It" for a flavor of this influential, era-defining album.

Innervisions/Stevie Wonder (1973)
Produced and engineered by: Robert Margouleff, Malcolm Cecil, and Stevie Wonder

This is a great reference album if you're in the middle of recording keys and you need some inspiration. Rhodes piano and Moog synths never sounded better than they do in this golden-era Stevie Wonder album. Essential listening.

Joe's Garage/Frank Zappa (1979)
Produced by: Frank Zappa
Engineer: Joe Chiccarelli

The inception of sound recording was the defining force and essence of 20th century music, so it makes sense that the greatest musician of the 20th century would also be the greatest exponent of sound recording and production. Whether Frank Zappa is the greatest composer and musician of the 20th century is debatable, but his incomparable skill as a self-proclaimed "studio wizard" is unequivocal. The sonic qualities of Joe's Garage will certainly not be to everyone's taste; there is no other album that sounds anything like it, even from within Zappa's own catalog. If you are a serious musician or producer, you must familiarize yourself with Zappa's work.

Kind Of Blue/Miles Davis (1959)
Produced and engineered by: Teo Macero and Irving Townsend

Was this the apex of jazz, the finest hour of a genre that would become increasingly irrelevant from that point onward? Who knows. This is one of the most influential recordings ever made, and it possesses huge atmosphere and vibe.

Pet Sounds/The Beach Boys (1966)
Produced by: Brian Wilson
Engineers: various

Brian Wilson is often credited as the first person to use the studio as a musical instrument, and *Pet Sounds* is universally recognized as his finest achievement. If you don't know this album already, what have you been doing!? If you do know it, dig it out again and marvel at its unique character and ingenuity.

The Queen Is Dead/ The Smiths (1986)
Produced by: Morrissey and Johnny Marr
Engineer: Stephen Street

On the whole, the aesthetic of recordings from the 1980s has not aged well, and any semblance of enduring appeal can be attributed to modern listeners' sense of kitsch and nostalgia. Foremost among the notable exceptions to this rule is *The Queen Is Dead*, a well-recorded album that has energy and a real "edge." In the UK, The Smiths are regarded as one of the best bands in recorded music history, and *The Queen Is Dead* is regularly voted "number one greatest album" of all time in those perennial music magazine hierarchies. If indie/rock is your thing, this is an indispensable album.

Sketches For My Sweetheart The Drunk/Jeff Buckley (1998)
Produced by: Nicholas Hill, Tom Verlaine, and Jeff Buckley
Engineers: various

Buckley's untimely death prevented this album from being completed. The tracks from studio sessions collected here are relatively uninteresting, but the four-track demos are a different story. Performed and recorded by Buckley at his home, they evince a level of originality and imagination sadly lacking from the vast majority of today's records. If you feel as though you've run out of inspiration, listen to this and be restored.

Speakerboxxx/The Love Below/Outkast (2003)
Produced by: Antwan Patton and Andre Benjamin
Engineers: various

Any album that sets out to be genre-busting is likely to have some interesting production going on. *Speakerboxxx...* is a peculiar album. It can't be defined as belonging to one genre unless you start some gratuitous word-splicing (alterna-hip-pop,

anyone?) and it certainly has some interesting moments of production and mixing in there. Weird and wonderful.

Steal This Album!/ System Of A Down (2002)
Produced by: Rick Rubin and Daron Malakian
Engineers: various

Rick Rubin is one of the biggest names in rock, having produced Metallica, Red Hot Chili Peppers, Rage Against The Machine, and Weezer among others. He is famous for getting great performances out of the bands he works with, sometimes at the expense of audio quality in the view of purists and audiophiles. There is some audible clipping and distortion on *Steal This Album!*, but it really doesn't matter. The important thing is the intensity of the performance, which is captured on this album brilliantly. Along with *Toxicity*, this album changed the course of modern metal.

The Stranger/Billy Joel (1977)
Produced by: Phil Ramone
Engineers: Jim Boyer and Phil Ramone

This is Billy Joel's most successful album, the product of a fertile creative relationship with Phil Ramone. Ramone began his career as a musician and is an accomplished violinist and composer in his own right; his list of production credits is impressive, including artists such as Ray Charles, Paul McCartney, James Taylor, and Elton John. An album with a fantastic sound and an unusually high ratio of hit songs to not-hit songs.

Thriller/Michael Jackson (1982)
Produced by: Quincy Jones and Michael Jackson
Engineer: Bruce Swedien

Those in the record industry who are intent of depriving music of all its character and dynamic range would do well to remind themselves that the most successful album of all time is, by audiophile standards, also one of the best-sounding pop albums ever produced. Thriller has real dynamic range and great sounds. Jackson, Jones, and Swedien triumphed with this one, an album you should always have handy as a reference.

True Blue/Madonna (1986)
Produced by: Stephen Bray, Patrick Leonard, and Madonna
Engineers: Michael Hutchinson and Michael Verdick

This playlist would be incomplete without an example of the archetypal 1980s pop production idiom. So here it is, *True Blue*. Play it through the best speakers you can find and you might be surprised to discover that it sounds rather good.
Key track
The bass sound on "La Isla Bonita" is quite addictive!

La Valse a Mille Temps/Jacques Brel (1959)

The English-speaking world has been a little slow to catch on, but Belgian singer-songwriter Jacques Brel is one of the all-time great recording artists. It doesn't matter if you don't speak French, you will still be able to appreciate the brilliance of Brel's delivery and Francois Rauber's perfectly judged orchestration.
Key track
"Les Flamandes" is the stand-out track.

Chapter 10

Useful information

A detailed glossary covering all the technical terms in the book, plus more, followed by resources: books, websites, and magazines that will help you on your way.

Glossary

A/D—Analog to digital.

album—See LP.

ampere—Unit of electrical current.

amplifier—Any device used to increase signal level can be described as an amplifier or amp.

analog—Circuitry designed to represent a signal (audio) as a continuously variable voltage.

attack—The initial phase of a sound.

attenuate—To decrease level. For example, "I used an EQ to attenuate the lower frequencies."

auto-tune—A digital pitch-shifting effect able to automatically correct out-of-tune audio.

aux send, aux return—Features on a typical mixing desk allowing signal to be sent to an external device and then returned to the desk from that device. For example, if you wanted to add delay to channels 3 and 7, you would engage the aux sends on those channels and route the sends to an external delay unit. The signal returning to the desk would come from the delay unit, and this could

be mixed with the original "dry" signal to taste. Aux is short for auxiliary.

balanced cable—A cable capable of eliminating unwanted noise and hum that might be introduced along its length by carrying two versions of the signal, one with its polarity inverted. In order for balanced cable to be effective it must be connected to balanced outputs and inputs.

Bandpass filter—Boosts or cuts frequencies around a specified frequency. Bandwidth determined by Q.

bandwidth—The range of frequencies an audio device is capable of producing or affecting.

bit—a binary digit. Also a switch with two positions, on (1) and off (0).

binary—A system of representation using only the digits 1 and 0.

bounce—Bouncing is the process of mixing several tracks down to one or two tracks, to free up tracks for further recording.

BPM—Beats per minute.

bus (or buss)—Signal path within a mixer to which signal from a channel or channels can be routed. The mix bus, for example, is the dual signal path to which all others are routed in a typical mixing setup.

byte—An ordered system of (typically) 8 bits. Shortened to B.

capacitance—The ability of a structure to hold electrical charge. Measured in Farad (F).

capacitor—Two conductive plates separated by an insulator. Capable of retaining electrical charge.

CD—Compact disc.

channel—On a mixing desk, a channel controls one input from a multitrack tape machine, DAW, or microphone.

chorus—An effect in which an audio signal is mixed with a delayed, pitch-modulated copy of itself.

click track—A metronomic click used during recording to keep musicians playing in time.

clipping—An ugly distortion produced when the level of audio signal exceeds the maximum level a piece of equipment is designed to handle.

coaxial—A common analog or digital audio connector.

compressor—A device capable of reducing dynamic range.

control room—The room in a studio from which mixing and monitoring is controlled.

conversion—The process of turning an electrical (analog) signal into a numeric (digital) one.

Cubase—Popular DAW.

current—The flow of electrical charge through a circuit. Measured in Ampere (A).

D/A—Digital to analog.

DAT—Digital Audio Tape.

demo—A demonstration of an unsigned act's music, typically containing three representative tracks, for the music industry's perusal.

DAW—Digital audio workstation.

dB (SPL)—Decibel. A measure of SPL ratio where 0dB is the threshold of human hearing.

dBU—Decibel (unloaded). Measure of signal ratio where 0dBU is 0.775V rms.

de-esser—A device capable of reducing sibilance in a vocal recording.

delay (effect)—A device that adds one or more time-delayed copies to the original signal.

delay (processor)—A device that replaces the original signal with a time-delayed copy of itself; used to combat phase cancellation between tracks.

DI—Direct injection, whereby a signal is introduced to a recording system directly from an instrument such as electric guitar or keyboard, without the use of a microphone.

digital—Data in binary form.

dry—A signal without added effects. When an aux send/return is introduced, for example, the signal becomes wet.

dynamics—The relative loudness of sound. If a musician is deciding whether to play a piece quietly or loudly, he is deciding an issue of dynamics.

dynamic range—The difference between the loudest and the quietest SPL, or signal level. Measured in dB.

EP—Extended play, a collection of about 15–30 minutes of songs.

equalizer (EQ)—A device for cutting or boosting certain frequencies.

fader—A sliding level control commonly found on mixing desks.

feedback—Noise created by the output signal looping back into the original input.

FET—Field Effect Transistor.

filter—Processor that boosts or cuts specified frequencies.

flanger—An effect in which an audio signal is mixed with a pitch-modulated copy of itself. Similar to chorus.

foldback—A foldback system allows performers in a studio to have different mixes sent to their headphones as they perform, and it allows those in the control room to speak with performers via headphones.

frequency—The rate of repetition of periodic motion. Measured in Hertz.

fundamental—The lowest frequency in a harmonic series. With rare exceptions, any note played on any instrument contains a fundamental.

gain—Measures the amount of amplitude applied to a signal.

gate—A device that mutes a signal when it falls below a user-defined threshold.

ground loop—A common problem in studios, in which electricity from the mains creates a hum by interfering with audio cabling.

group—When a selection of tracks are routed to a single fader or pair of faders, they become a group, controllable from that fader or pair of faders.

harmonic—A frequency within a signal that is an integer multiple of the fundamental frequency.

harmonic distortion— When audio equipment such as a tube compressor adds extra harmonics to a signal, this is known as harmonic distortion.

headroom—The amount (measured in dB) by which the signal capabilities of a system exceed an actual signal level.

High-pass filter—Only lets frequencies above specified frequency pass unaltered.

Hz—Short for Hertz, the unit with which frequency is measured.

IC—Integrated circuit.

impedance—A measure of opposition to a sinusoidal alternating current within a circuit. Measured in Ohm (Ω). Also referred to as resistance.

insert—When an effect or processor is patched into an insert point on a mixer, the processed signal supersedes and replaces the original. This contrasts with a "send" effect in which dry and wet versions of a signal are usually mixed.

ips—Inches per second, a measure of tape speed.

ITB—In the box, a term referring to processing and mixing conducted entirely in a DAW.

jack—A connector, like the one found on an electric guitar lead.

kHz—1000 Hz.

LDC—Large-diaphragm condenser microphone.

limiter—A device used to prevent the signal level exceeding a user-defined threshold.

line level—The standard signal level that signal processors

such as mixing desks and compressors are designed to accommodate.

Logic—Popular DAW.

low-pass filter—Only lets frequencies below specified frequency pass unaltered.

LP—Long Play, a collection of songs lasting between 30 and 80 minutes.

mic level—Refers to the level of signal generated by a microphone before it is amplified by a preamp to line level.

microphone—Device that transduces sound waves into electrical current.

MIDI—Musical Instrument Digital Interface.

mixer, mixing desk, mixing console—A device for combining audio signals and adjusting their relative levels.

monitor—A speaker designed for studio use.

mono—Single-channel sound reproduction and recording. Short for "monaural."

multitrack recording—The process of recording an ensemble onto several tracks.

nearfield—A studio monitor designed to be listened to at relatively close quarters.

Nuendo—A DAW.

Ohm (Ω)—Unit in which impedance and resistance is measured.

overdub—The practice of adding further parts to a multi-track recording.

overdrive—Feeding a device more amplitude than it is designed to handle. Often used on tube amplifiers for effect.

pad—A common feature on preamps, a pad allows the user to reduce the incoming signal level from a microphone to prevent clipping.

pan—Position tracks within the stereo field.

patch bay—A cabling solution used by most professional studios; a central point from which everything can be routed.

peak—A sharp relative maximum in the signal level.

phantom power—A power supply (typically 48V) which can be carried by balanced audio cable from preamp to microphone.

phaser—An effect; combines a phase-shifted version of a signal with the original signal.

pickup—The part of an electric guitar or bass responsible for picking up vibrations from strings and converting these into an electrical signal.

pitch shifter—A digital process capable of changing the pitch of a signal while leaving its duration unaffected.

plugin—A software tool that works inside a DAW, such as an audio effect or processor.

pop shield—Device placed between microphone and singer that filters out plosives.

power (electric)—The product of voltage and electrical current. Measured in Watt (W).

post-fader—Applies when an aux send is configured in such a way that changes in the relevant channel's overall (fader) level affects the level of signal being "sent" to the aux output.

preamp—A device that brings an electrical signal from microphone level to line level.

pre-fader—Applies when an aux send is configured in such a way that changes in the relevant channel's overall (fader) level will not affect the level of signal being "sent" to the aux output.

Pro Tools—Industry standard DAW.

optical—A low-loss digital audio connector.

OTB—Out of the box, a term referring to processing and mixing conducted outside of a DAW, i.e. outboard processors.

Q—Describes the bandwidth of a band-pass filter.

quantize—To move notes (especially in MIDI) to a predetermined temporal location in each bar, for example, every sixteenth note. If something is quantized it should be perfectly in time.

Radar—DAW and hardware interface.

RAM—Random access memory.

reverb—The echoes and reflections of a sound from, for example, the walls, ceiling, floor, and contents of a normal room. The term can apply to both naturally occurring reverberations and artificial reverbs.

sample—A digitally stored sound recording used or intended to be used in a context different to the one in which it was originally recorded.

SDC—Small-diaphragm condenser microphone.

sequencer—A device for recording and editing

MIDI data. Sometimes the terms sequencer and DAW are used interchangeably because some computer sequencers, such as Cubase and Logic, did evolve into DAWs.

side-chain—Allows a circuit to respond to a signal other than the one it is processing.

signal—Sound in its analogous electrical form.

solid-state—Method of amplification using a transistor.

Sonar—A DAW.

SPL—Sound pressure level, measured in decibels.

stereo—Double-channel sound reproduction and recording. Short for stereophonic sound.

tempo—The speed of a piece of music, measured in BPM.

transients—Frequencies that occur only during the initial attack phase.

Transistor—Semi-conductor device for amplifying an electrical signal.

THD—Total harmonic distortion.

Track—(1) One recording of sound that forms part of a multitrack recording. (2) A song.

tracking—Recording.

TS—Tip, sleeve. A common cable connector.

TRS—Tip, ring, sleeve. A common cable connector.

Tube—Thermionic device used to amplify an electrical signal consisting of several components in a vacuum encased in glass.

tweeter—A small loudspeaker for reproducing high frequencies. Forms part of a monitor.

unbalanced cable—A common sort of cable, one without the hum-canceling ability of balanced cable.

USB—Universal serial bus. A serial bus standard to connect devices to a PC or Mac.

Volt—see voltage.

voltage—The difference in charge levels between two conductive elements. Measured in Volts (V).

VU meter—A visualization of signal level.

Watt—Unit of power.

woofer—A loudspeaker that reproduces lower frequencies. Part of a monitor speaker.

XLR—A common three-pronged cable connector, usually used to carry a balanced signal.

XY positioning—Two microphones with diaphragms on the same vertical plane facing in different directions.

Prefix factors			
Prefix	Derived from	Factor	Typically found in
μ (micro)	*Mikros* (Greek): "small"	One millionth: 0.000001	Capacitance (μF)
m (milli)	*Mille* (Latin): "one thousand"	One thousandth: 0.001	Voltage (mV), Power (mW), Current (mA)
d (deci)	*Decimus* (Latin): "one tenth"	One tenth: 0.1	dB
k (kilo)	*Khilioi* (Greek): "one thousand"	One thousand: 1,000	Impedance (kΩ), Audio frequency (kHz)
M (mega)	*Megas* (Greek): "great"	One million: 1,000,000	CPU speed (MHz), RAM (MB), digital conversion rate (MHz)
G (giga)	*Gigas* (Greek): "giant"	One billion: 1,000,000,000	Hard disk capacity (GB)
T (tera)	*Teras* (Greek): "monster"	One trillion: 1,000,000,000,000	Hard disk (TB)

Resources

Web

http://www.gearslutz.com/board/
The ultimate recording gear junky's forum!

http://www.tapeop.com/
Old-school sound engineers' hangout. Full of useful information, technical advice, and recording tips.

http://mixonline.com/
An online recording magazine, full of interviews, reviews, and recording news.

http://www.prosoundweb.com/
Check out the forums, which are particularly useful!

http://www.prodigy-pro.com/diy/index.php
If you intend to build your own recording gear one day, this is a forum you need to visit.

http://www.myspaceskins.com/
One of the best sites for customizing your MySpace page quickly and impressively.

http://www.thenewmusicsite.com
An interesting take on online music promotion for unsigned acts that's worth checking out—excellent for building fan databases!

http://www.homestead.com, http://www.webs.com
Offers free customizable templates for your webpage, and free hosting!

Books and magazines

Mastering Audio: The Art and the Science by Bob Katz (second edition)
Perhaps the best book about professional audio out there. Mastering is the subject, but this book should be read by everyone involved in recording.

Sound On Sound
An internationally respected British home recording magazine.

TapeOp
A fantastic publication; impartial, detailed, and everything a magazine about recording should be. Go to the TapeOp website to subscribe and you may be pleasantly surprised by the price!

Behind The Glass by Howard Massey
Interviews with just about every big name producer around. Enlightening stuff, with plenty of trade secrets revealed.

The Real Frank Zappa by Frank Zappa
Tales from the weird side of the music industry from the great composer/ producer himself.

Handbook for Sound Engineers by Glen Ballou (third edition)
Serious, thorough, and technical, this is an excellent reference book for aspiring sound engineers.

Build your own website the right way using HTML and CSS by Ian Lloyd
HTML and CSS are the backbone of every good webpage. This book shows you how to structure your code tidily and efficiently.

Index

Picture credits

Quarto would like to thank
the following agencies, for
kindly supplying images for
inclusion in this book:

Getty Images: pp. 10, 15, 23,
24, 55, 131, 133, 166

Rex Features: p.28

www.shutterstock.com
www.istockphotos.com
www.wikipedia.com

p.79, Brendan Biele/www.
flickr.com

We would also like to
thank the following
manufacturers for kindly
supplying images:
www.audio-technica.co.uk
Copyright Audio-Technica
Ltd
www.neumann.com
Georg Neumann GmbH
www.ams-neve.com
Neve 1073 photo(s) courtesy
of AMS Neve Ltd
www.chameleonlabs.com
www.manleylabs.com
Manley Variable Mu®
www.adam-audio.com
www.klein-hummel.com
www.mun.ca/music

All other images are
the copyright of Quarto
Publishing plc. While
every effort has been made
to credit contributors,
Quarto would like to apolo-
gize should there have been
any omissions or errors—
and would be pleased to
make the appropriate cor-
rection for future editions of
the book.